Advancing Maths for AQA
STATISTICS 3 & 6

Gill Buqué

Series editors
Roger Williamson   Sam Boardman
Ted Graham   Keith Parramore

Heinemann Educational Publishers
a division of Heinemann Publishers (Oxford) Ltd,
Halley Court, Jordan Hill, Oxford OX2 8EJ

OXFORD   MELBOURNE   AUCKLAND   JOHANNESBURG
BLANTYRE   GABORONE   PORTSMOUTH NH (USA)   CHICAGO

First published in 2001

05   04   03   02   01
10   9   8   7   6   5   4   3   2   1

ISBN 0 435 51314 1

Cover design by Miller, Craig and Cocking

Typeset and illustrated by Tech-Set Limited, Gateshead, Tyne & Wear

Printed and bound by Scotprint in the UK

Acknowledgements
The publishers and authors acknowledge the work of the writers, David Cassell,
Ian Hardwick, Mary Rouncefield, David Burghes, Ann Ault and Nigel Price of
the *AEB Mathematics for AS and A-Level Series*, from which some exercises and
examples have been taken.

The publishers' and authors' thanks are due to the AQA for permission to
reproduce questions from past examination papers.

The answers have been provided by the authors and are not the responsibility
of the examining board.

About this book

This book is one in a series of textbooks designed to provide you with exceptional preparation for AQA's new Advanced GCE Specification B. The series authors are all senior members of the examining team and have prepared the textbooks specifically to support you in studying this course.

Finding your way around

The following are there to help you find your way around when you are studying and revising:

- **edge marks** (shown on the front page) – these help you to get to the right chapter quickly;
- **contents list** – this identifies the individual sections dealing with key syllabus concepts so that you can go straight to the areas that you are looking for;
- **index** – a number in bold type indicates where to find the main entry for that topic.

Key points

Key points are not only summarised at the end of each chapter but are also boxed and highlighted within the text like this:

> If A and B are two events then A ∪ B or the **union** of A and B is defined as 'A or B' which is the combined event 'at least one of A and B occurs'.

Exercises and exam questions

Worked examples and carefully graded questions familiarise you with the specification and bring you up to exam standard. Each book contains:

- Worked examples and worked exam questions to show you how to tackle typical questions; examiner's tips will also provide guidance;
- Graded exercises, gradually increasing in difficulty up to exam-level questions, which are marked by an [A];
- Test-yourself sections for each chapter so that you can check your understanding of the key aspects of that chapter and identify any sections that you should review;
- Answers to the questions are included at the end of the book.

Contents

Introduction

S3 and S6 are two units with the same syllabus. The examination for S3 is set at AS level and the examination for S6 is set at A2 level. All the examples in this book lie within the syllabus. The dividing line between an S3 question and an S6 question is somewhat blurred. However as a guideline questions marked * are more appropriate to S6 candidates.

The A2 nature of a question may only lie in the last parts and so many of the * questions will have parts which are accessible to average S3 candidates. The other questions will also provide useful practice for S6 candidates.

CHAPTER I

Further probability

Learning objectives

After studying this chapter you should be able to:

- evaluate probabilities of combined events in a variety of circumstances
- apply the laws
  $P(A \cup B) = P(A) + P(B) - P(A \cap B)$
  $P(A \cap B) = P(A)P(B \mid A)$
- evaluate conditional probabilities using

$$P(A \mid B) = \frac{P(A \cap B)}{P(B)}$$

In S1, Chapter 4, the concept of probability was introduced. In this book, the techniques will be extended.

1.1 Unions and intersections

If A and B are two events then $A \cup B$ or the **union** of A and B is defined as 'A or B' which is the combined event 'at least one of A and B occurs'.

In Statistics 1, 4.4, $P(A \cup B)$ is examined for mutually exclusive events. In this book, $P(A \cup B)$ will be found for events which are not mutually exclusive.

The **intersection** $A \cap B$ is defined as 'A and B' which is the combined event that 'both A and B occur'. Clearly, $P(A \cap B) = 0$ when A and B are mutually exclusive.

The general formula for the probability of the union of two events A and B is:

$$P(A \cup B) = P(A) + P(B) - P(A \cap B)$$

This is an important probability law but counting equally likely outcomes to find combined probabilities, as used in S1, will usually be an easier method. This is also the recommended method in S3.

An example is given to illustrate the above law but remember that this question can also be solved by counting equally likely outcomes.

Worked example 1.1

The following table gives the numbers of full-time male and female students enrolled on a variety of courses at a Further Education college in 1999.

	Male	Female
IT	56	64
GCSE/GCE	113	134
GNVQ	34	44
Construction	56	9
Engineering	43	17
Business	54	46
Languages	12	18

It is always sensible to find the totals for each group in the table first.

	M	F	Total
IT	56	64	**120**
GC	113	134	**247**
GN	34	44	**78**
Con	56	9	**65**
Eng	43	17	**60**
Bus	54	46	**100**
Lan	12	18	**30**
Total	**368**	**332**	**700**

One of the students is selected at random.
A is the event 'a female student is selected'.
B is the event 'an Engineering student is selected'.
C is the event 'a GCSE/GCE student is selected'.
D is the event 'a Language student is selected'.

Find the following probabilities:

(a) $P(A)$; (b) $P(A \cap B)$; (c) $P(B \cup C)$;
(d) $P(A \cup D)$; (e) $P(C \cup A)$.

Solution

(a) $P(A)$ = probability a student selected at random is female

$$= \frac{332}{700} = \frac{83}{175} \text{ or } 0.474$$

Considering the totals in the table, there are 332 females out of the 700 students.

(b) $P(A \cap B)$ = probability both **A and B** occur
= probability a student selected at random is a female engineering student

$$= \frac{17}{700} \text{ or } 0.0243$$

Clearly from the table, there are 17 female engineering students.

(c) $P(B \cup C)$ = probability **B or C or both** occur
= probability a student selected at random is either an engineering student or a GCSE/GCE student or both

It is not possible for a student to be an engineering student and a GCSE/GCE student. They are either one or the other.

B and C are clearly mutually exclusive events so
$P(B \cup C) = P(B) + P(C)$

$$= \frac{60}{700} + \frac{247}{700} = \frac{307}{700} \text{ or } 0.439$$

(d) $\text{P}(A \cup D)$ = probability **A or D or both** occur
= probability a student selected at random is either female or a languages student or both

A and D are **not** mutually exclusive events so
$\text{P}(A \cup D) = \text{P}(A) + \text{P}(D) - \text{P}(A \cap D)$

$$= \frac{332}{700} + \frac{30}{700} - \frac{18}{700} = \frac{344}{700} = \frac{86}{175} \text{ or } 0.491 \text{ (3 sf)}$$

> Care must be taken not to include the 18 female languages students twice. These students are counted in A and in D hence $\text{P}(A \cap D)$ is subtracted from $\text{P}(A) + \text{P}(D)$.

Alternatively, the answer can be obtained by considering the table and totalling:

$$\text{P}(A \cup D) = \frac{64 + 134 + 44 + 9 + 17 + 46 + 18 + 12}{700}$$

$$= \frac{344}{700} \text{ as above}$$

> Note that is just as easy to count equally likely outcomes to find $\text{P}(A \cup D)$ as explained in S1.

(e) Using the same methods as in **(d)** since C and A are also not mutually exclusive:
$\text{P}(C \cup A) = \text{P}(C) + \text{P}(A) - \text{P}(C \cap A)$

$$= \frac{247}{700} + \frac{332}{700} - \frac{134}{700} = \frac{445}{700} = \frac{89}{140} \text{ or } 0.636 \text{ (3 sf)}$$

Alternatively

$$\text{P}(C \cup A) = \frac{113 + 134 + 64 + 44 + 9 + 17 + 46 + 18}{700}$$

$$= \frac{445}{700} \text{ as above}$$

$$= 0.636$$

> The answer can be seen by totalling the relevant numbers directly from the table:
>
> | | M | F | Total |
> |-------|-----|-----|-------|
> | IT | 56 | 64 | 120 |
> | GC | 113 | 134 | 247 |
> | GN | 34 | 44 | 78 |
> | Con | 56 | 9 | 65 |
> | Eng | 43 | 17 | 60 |
> | Bus | 54 | 46 | 100 |
> | Lan | 12 | 18 | 30 |
> | Total | 368 | 332 | 700 |

Worked example 1.2

Twenty interviews with members of a Sports Club were carried out. Of the 12 men interviewed, eight preferred working out in the gym to organised fitness groups. Of the eight women interviewed, three preferred working out in the gym.

A person is chosen at random from these 20 people. What is the probability that the person is either a woman or a person who preferred working out in the gym?

Solution

Let's call the event that a selected person is female, F, and the event that a selected person prefers the gym, G.

We require $P(F \cup G) = P(F) + P(G) - P(F \cap G)$.

Clearly, $P(F) = \dfrac{8}{20}$ as there are eight women involved and

$P(G) = \dfrac{8+3}{20} = \dfrac{11}{20}$ as eight men and three women preferred the gym.

The event $(F \cap G)$ represents a person who is female and who prefers the gym. Hence $P(F \cap G) = \dfrac{3}{20}$ since three females preferred the gym.

This gives $P(F \cup G) = \dfrac{8}{20} + \dfrac{11}{20} - \dfrac{3}{20} = \dfrac{16}{20} = \dfrac{4}{5}$ or 0.8.

The counting method would involve forming a table:

	Gym	Org. fit	Total
Male	8	4	12
Female	3	5	8
Total	11	9	20

So $P(F \cup G) = \dfrac{8+3+5}{20}$

EXERCISE IA

1 At a school, children can join lunchtime clubs. The following table gives the numbers of children, male and female, attending clubs on a Monday.

	Male	Female
Art	7	12
Sport	18	7
Computer	10	6

One of these children is selected at random.
A is the event 'the child attends Art club'.
B is the event 'the child is female'.
C is the event 'the child attends Computer club'.

Find the following probabilities:

(a) $P(A)$; (b) $P(B)$;

(c) $P(A \cap B)$; (d) $P(A \cup C)$;

(e) $P(A \cup B)$; (f) $P(B \cup C)$;

(g) $P(B \cap C)$.

2 In a Statistics class, a group of 25 students were given two problems to solve. The first, easy problem resulted in 21 correct answers but only 15 students correctly solved the second, more complex problem. In the whole class, only 13 solved both problems correctly. Find the probability that a student chosen at random from this class solved at least one of the problems correctly.

*3 An orchestra has 150 members. There are 60 male members, 15 of whom play in the string section. There are 25 male members in the woodwind section.

The probability that a member selected at random from this orchestra is in the string section is 0.4 and the corresponding probability for the woodwind section is 0.3.

If the events S, M and W are defined as,
S is the event 'member is in string section'.
M is the event 'member is male'.
W is the event 'member is in woodwind section'.

Find the following probabilities,

(a) P(M);

(b) P(M ∩ S);

(c) P(M ∪ W);

(d) P(S ∩ W);

(e) a member selected at random is a female in the string section;

(f) a member selected at random is a female in the woodwind section. [A]

4 Two digits X and Y are chosen from a table of random sampling digits (i.e. from 0, 1, 2, ..., 9). The event R is that $X = Y + 1$ and the event S is that X and Y are both less than 2. Find:

(a) P(R);

(b) P(R ∩ S);

(c) P(R ∪ S).

*5 In a group of 200 office workers, the probability that a worker chosen at random is male is $\frac{2}{5}$ and the probability that he or she wears glasses is $\frac{1}{5}$.

It is known that 20 of the male office workers in this group wear glasses.

If A is defined as the event 'a worker chosen at random is male' and event G is defined as 'a worker chosen at random wears glasses'.

Find:

(a) P(A ∩ G);

(b) P(A ∪ G);

(c) Define the two events (A ∩ G) and (A ∪ G) in words. [A]

1.2 Independence

In S1, Section 4.5, the concept of independent events was introduced and the law

$$P(A \cap B) = P(A) \cdot P(B)$$

was used.

This law can be extended to any number of independent events, so, for example

$$P(A \cap B \cap C \cap D \cap E) = P(A) \cdot P(B) \cdot P(C) \cdot P(D) \cdot P(E)$$

This law was used in numerical examples in S1.

Worked example 1.3

Dipa orders a mini hi-fi system from Galaxy Electronics. The system consists of speakers, an amplifier and a CD player. It is known that the probability that the speakers will have a fault is 0.02, the probability the amplifier has a fault is 0.03 and the probability that the CD player is faulty is 0.05 and that these probabilities are independent.

What is the probability that Dipa's new hi-fi has:

(a) all three parts working correctly,

(b) only one part not working correctly?

From the information given, the probabilities are:
$P(A) = 0.02$,
$P(B) = 0.03$,
$P(C) = 0.05$.

Solution

Let A be the event 'speakers have a fault'.
Let B be the event 'amplifier has a fault'.
Let C be the event 'CD player has a fault'.

The event 'speakers do not have a fault' is denoted A′ and is called the **complement** of event A.

The event 'amplifier does not have a fault' is denoted B′ and is called the **complement** of event B.

The event 'CD player does not have a fault' is denoted C′ and is called the **complement** of event C.

From above, clearly the complementary events A′, B′, C′ have probabilities:
$P(A') = 1 - P(A) = 0.98$
$P(B') = 1 - P(B) = 0.97$
$P(C') = 1 - P(C) = 0.95$.

(a) P(all three work correctly)
$$= P(A' \cap B' \cap C') = P(A') \cdot P(B') \cdot P(C')$$
$$= 0.98 \times 0.97 \times 0.95 = 0.903$$

(b) The combined event 'only **one** not working correctly' is made up of three mutually exclusive events. These are:

$$A \cap B' \cap C' \text{ and } A' \cap B \cap C' \text{ and } A' \cap B' \cap C$$

So P(only one not working correctly
$$= P(A \cap B' \cap C') + P(A' \cap B \cap C') + P(A' \cap B' \cap C)$$
$$= (0.02 \times 0.97 \times 0.95) + (0.98 \times 0.03 \times 0.95)$$
$$+ (0.98 \times 0.97 \times 0.05)$$
$$= 0.0939$$

The events are:
speakers not working but amplifier and CD are OK, amplifier not working but speakers and CD are OK, or CD not working but speakers and amplifiers are OK.

Worked example 1.4

In a family with two children, the father decides that he will offer to play a popular board game with his children one evening. They are delighted to take up his offer.

From past experience, the father knows that the independent probabilities that his son, his daughter or he himself will accumulate over £10 000 by the end of the game are 0.6, 0.4 and 0.7, respectively.

Find the probability that, at the end of the game:

(a) all three have over £10 000;

(b) only the son has over £10 000;

(c) two of the three players have over £10 000.

Solution

(a) P(all three) = P(son has) . P(daughter has) . P(father has)
$$= 0.6 \times 0.4 \times 0.7 = 0.168;$$

> A tree diagram could be used.

(b) P(son only) = P(son has) . P(daughter not) . P(father not)
$$= 0.6 \times 0.6 \times 0.3 = 0.108$$

(c) P(only two have) is made up of three mutually exclusive combined events
Son and daughter have, father does not
Son and father have, daughter does not
Daughter and father have, son does not
Hence, P(only two) $= (0.6 \times 0.4 \times 0.3)$
$$+ (0.6 \times 0.7 \times 0.6)$$
$$+ (0.4 \times 0.7 \times 0.4) = 0.436$$

EXERCISE 1B

1 A girl travels to school by bus. The bus route includes a drive down a main road which has three roundabouts. The roundabouts are positioned at three busy intersections and the probability that the bus has to stop at the first roundabout is 0.6, at the second the probability is 0.9 and at the third, 0.7. The probability of having to stop at any one roundabout is independent of the probability of having to stop at any other roundabout. Find the probability that:

(a) the bus has to stop at all three roundabouts;

(b) the bus has to stop at only one of the three roundabouts.

2 Vehicles approaching a crossroad must go in one of three directions – left, right or straight on. Observations by traffic engineers showed that of vehicles approaching from the north; 45% turn left, 20% turn right and 35% go straight on.

Assuming that each driver chooses independently, what is the probability that, of the next three vehicles approaching from the north,

(a) all go straight on;

(b) all go in the same direction;

(c) two turn left and one goes straight on? [A]

3 A group of three school friends, Jane, Amy and Alisha, normally eat a packed lunch but each of the friends always asks their parents for some money to buy a school lunch in the canteen on a Friday.

The probability that Jane's parents will agree to giving her money is 0.5, and the corresponding probabilities for Amy and Alisha are 0.3 and 0.8, respectively.

The parents decide independently of each other.

Find the probability that, on a given Friday:

(a) all three get money for a school lunch;

(b) all three are not allowed money for a school lunch;

(c) only one of the three friends is not allowed money for a school lunch. [A]

4 A pharmaceutical company carries out three separate checks on bottles of sedative solution.

The checks are entirely independent of each other and involve monitoring correct labelling and the secure fastening of the safety lid and also an assessment of the volume of the solution in each bottle.

The probability that a bottle fails the labelling check is 0.2, the probability that it fails the lid security check is 0.08 and the probability that the volume level is unacceptable is 0.05.

For a randomly selected bottle, what is the probability that:

(a) it fails all three checks;

(b) it fails on labelling but passes the other two checks;

(c) it fails on just one of the checks;

(d) it is passed as satisfactory on all three checks? [A]

5 A roadside police check is set up and cars are pulled over at random and assessed for the safety of three features: tyres, brakes and lights.

The probability that any car fails the tyre safety check is 0.12, the probability it fails on brakes is 0.06 and the probability it fails the light checks is 0.17.

Assuming these probabilities are independent, find the probability that a car:

(a) passes all three checks;

(b) fails on the lights check only;

(c) fails on two features. [A]

1.3 Conditional probability

In S1, Section 4.7, the concept of conditional probability is introduced.

> The notation P(A | B) is used for the **conditional** probability that event A occurs given that it is known that event B occurs (or has occurred).

> The general rule for the probability of the intersection of two events is
>
> $$P(A \cap B) = P(A) \cdot P(B \mid A)$$
> $$\text{or} = P(B) \cdot P(A \mid B)$$

This rule also leads to the general rule for conditional probability which is given below.

This rule applies to events which may or may not be made up of equally likely outcomes.

> $$P(A \mid B) = \frac{P(A \cap B)}{P(B)}$$

> For independent events A and B:
>
> $$P(A \mid B) = P(A)$$
>
> and
>
> $$P(B \mid A) = P(B)$$

Worked example 1.5

The two events A and B are such that P(A) = 0.6 P(B) = 0.2 and P(A | B) = 0.1

Calculate the probabilities that:

(a) both events A and B occur;

(b) at least one of the events A or B occur;

(c) B occurs, given that A is known to have occurred.

Solution

(a) $P(A \cap B)$ is required
$P(A \cap B) = P(B) \cdot P(A \mid B) = 0.2 \times 0.1 = 0.02$

(b) $P(A \cup B)$ is required
$P(A \cup B) = P(A) + P(B) - P(A \cap B)$
$\qquad = 0.6 + 0.2 - 0.02 = 0.78$

(c) $P(B \mid A)$ is required

$P(B \mid A) = \dfrac{P(A \cap B)}{P(A)}$

$\qquad = \dfrac{0.02}{0.6} = \dfrac{1}{30} = 0.0333$

Worked example 1.6

After advertising for an assistant, a shop manager decided to interview suitable applicants.

The interviews will either be in the morning or in the afternoon with probabilities 0.45 and 0.55, respectively. Each applicant is contacted by telephone and, in each case, a message has to be left. The probability that a morning interview is incorrectly transmitted to the applicant as an afternoon interview is 0.2 and the probability that an afternoon interview is incorrectly transmitted as a morning interview is 0.1.

Find the probability that:

(a) an applicant is selected for a morning interview and arrives for a morning interview;

(b) an applicant arrives at the correct time of day for their interview.

Solution

Let event M be 'selected for morning interview'.
Let event N be 'selected for afternoon interview'.
Let event C be 'correct information transmitted'.
We know that $P(M) = 0.45 \qquad P(N) = 0.55$
$\qquad\qquad P(C \mid M) = 0.8 \quad P(C \mid N) = 0.9$

(a) this requires $P(M) \times P(C \mid M)$

$\qquad = 0.45 \times 0.8 = 0.36$

(b) we need the two mutually exclusive events :

'a morning applicant correctly arriving in the morning'
'an afternoon applicant correctly arriving in the afternoon' for interview

$P(\text{correct}) = P(M) \times P(C \mid M) + P(N) \times P(C \mid N)$
$\qquad = (0.45 \times 0.8) + (0.55 \times 0.9)$
$\qquad = 0.855$

In this case, the only two possibilities are that an applicant has an interview in the morning or one in the afternoon.

Hence,
P(turns up at correct time) = P(morning).P(correct | morning) + P(afternoon) . P(correct | afternoon)

1.4 Total probability theorem

In Example **1.6(b)** the probability that an applicant arrives at the correct time is found by considering the only two possible ways for this event to occur. This is an example of the **total probability theorem**.

There may only be two mutually exclusive events as in Example **1.6(b)** or there may be more than two. In this module, it is unlikely that more than three would be involved.

> As an example, for three separate mutually exclusive and exhaustive events B_1, B_2 and B_3 the **total probability theorem** tells us that:
>
> $$P(A) = P(B_1) \cdot P(A \mid B_1)$$
> $$+ P(B_2) \cdot P(A \mid B_2)$$
> $$+ P(B_3) \cdot P(A \mid B_3)$$

Worked example 1.7

Climbing rope for use by mountaineers is tested for strength. A safety testing centre receives such rope from three different suppliers: 20% of its tests are carried out on samples of rope from supplier A; 30% from supplier B; 50% from supplier C.

From past experience, the probability of failing the strength test is 0.04 for a sample from A, 0.16 for a sample from B and 0.08 for a sample from C.

Find the probability that a randomly selected strength test will result in a failure.

Solution

In this case there are three separate mutually exclusive and exhaustive events to consider. These are:

    'rope from supplier A'
    'rope from supplier B'
    'rope from supplier C'.

The total probability theorem tells us that
$$P(\text{failure}) = P(A) \cdot P(\text{fail} \mid A) + P(B) \cdot P(\text{fail} \mid B) + P(C) \cdot P(\text{fail} \mid C)$$

In this case, $P(\text{strength test results in failure})$
$$= (0.20 \times 0.04) + (0.30 \times 0.16) + (0.50 \times 0.08) = 0.096$$

1.5 Bayes' theorem

In the problems considered so far which involve conditional probabilities, the questions all involved the evaluation of the probability that event A will occur, given that it is known that event B has already occurred. A and B may in fact happen at the same time but it is usually easier to think of one happening before the other.

The simplified version of Bayes' theorem which will be required for evaluation of conditional probabilities is:

$$P(B \mid A) = \frac{P(A \cap B)}{P(A)}$$

The 'reverse' problem will now be considered. This involves finding the probability that, given event A occurs, it was **preceded** by event B.

In Example 1.7, a problem of this type could be to find the probability that a rope which failed the strength test had been supplied by *C*.

P(supplied by *C* | failed strength test)

$$= \frac{P(\text{supplied by } C \cap \text{failed strength test})}{P(\text{failed strength test})}$$

Using results already obtained, the required probability

$$= \frac{0.50 \times 0.08}{0.096} = 0.417 \left(\text{or } \frac{5}{12}\right).$$

In the earlier Example 1.6, a problem of this type could be to find the probability that an applicant who turns up in the afternoon for an interview, was originally intended to be invited in the afternoon for an interview.

P(selected for afternoon | turned up in afternoon)

$$= \frac{P(\text{afternoon selected} \cap \text{message correct for afternoon})}{P(\text{turned up in afternoon})}$$

The event 'turned up in the afternoon' involves two, mutually exclusive combined events:

'intended for morning and message incorrect'
'intended for afternoon and message correct'.

Therefore the required probability is
P(turned up in afternoon)

$$= P(M) \times P(C' \mid M) + P(N) \times P(C \mid N)$$
$$= (0.45 \times 0.2) + (0.55 \times 0.9) = 0.585$$

The general form of Bayes' theorem is more complicated and extends conditional probability to considering several alternative previous events.

You will only need to use the simplified formula:

$$P(B \mid A) = \frac{P(A \cap B)}{P(A)}$$

where event A will involve two or more mutually exclusive events.
$P(A \cap B)$ is often found by using $P(A \cap B) = P(B) \cdot P(A \mid B)$ and $P(A)$ by using the **total probability theorem**.

N is event 'selected for afternoon interview'.
M is event 'selected for morning interview'.

In this case, the probability of the event 'turned up in afternoon', using the **total probability theorem**, is found from,
$P(M) \cdot P(\text{turned up afternoon} \mid M) + P(N) \cdot P(\text{turned up afternoon} \mid N)$

C is the event 'message correct'.
C' is the event 'message is incorrect'.

So the probability that a person who turns up in the afternoon was originally intended to have an afternoon interview

$$= \frac{0.55 \times 0.9}{0.585} = 0.846$$

Worked example 1.8

A vehicle insurance company classifies drivers as *A*, *B* or *C* according to whether or not they are a good risk, a medium risk or a poor risk with regard to having an accident. The company estimates that *A* constitutes 30% of drivers who are insured and *B* constitutes 50%. The probability that a class *A* driver will have one or more accidents in any 12-month period is 0.01, the corresponding values for *B* and *C* being 0.03 and 0.06, respectively.

(a) Find the probability that a motorist, chosen at random, is assessed as a class *C* risk and will have one or more accidents in a 12-month period.

(b) Find the probability that a motorist, chosen at random, will have one or more accidents in a 12-month period.

(c) The company sells a policy to a customer and within 12 months the customer has an accident. Find the probability that the customer is a class *C* risk.

Solution

P(*A*) = 0.30   P(*B*) = 0.50   P(*C*) = 0.20
Let X be the event 'driver has one or more accidents'.
P(X | *A*) = 0.01   P(X | *B*) = 0.03   P(X | *C*) = 0.06.

(a) $P(C \cap X) = P(C) \cdot P(X \mid C) = 0.20 \times 0.06 = 0.012$

(b) P(one or more accidents) is made up of three mutually exclusive events:
'Motorist is classified *A* and has accident'.
'Motorist is classified *B* and has accident'.
'Motorist is classified *C* and has accident'.
So P(X) = P(*A*) . P(X | *A*) + P(*B*) . P(X | *B*) + P(*C*) . P(X | *C*)
$= (0.30 \times 0.01) + (0.50 \times 0.03) + (0.20 \times 0.06)$
$= 0.03$

(c) $P(C \mid \text{had one or more accidents}) = \dfrac{P(C \cap X)}{P(X)} = \dfrac{0.012}{0.03} = 0.4$

Worked example 1.9

Conveyor belting for use in mines is tested for both strength and safety (the safety test is based on the amount of heat generated if the belt snaps). A testing station receives belting from three different suppliers: 30% of its tests are carried out on samples of belting from supplier *A*; 45% from *B*; 25% from *C*. From past experience the probability of failing the strength test is 0.02 for a sample from *A*, 0.12 from *B* and 0.04 from *C*.

(a) What is the probability that a particular strength test will result in a failure?

(b) If a strength test results in a failure, what is the probability that the belting came from supplier *A*?

(c) What is the probability of a sample failing both strength and safety tests given the following further information:

Supplier *A*   the probability of failing the safety test is 0.05 and is independent of the probability of failing the strength test;

Supplier *B*   1% of samples fail both strength and safety tests;

Supplier *C*   exactly half the samples which fail the strength test also fail the safety test.

Solution

$P(A) = 0.30$ $P(B) = 0.45$ $P(C) = 0.25$
Let F be the event 'belt fails strength test'.
So $P(F \mid A) = 0.02$ $P(F \mid B) = 0.12$ $P(F \mid C) = 0.04$.

(a) P(Fail strength test)
$$= P(\text{from } A \text{ and fail}) + P(\text{from } B \text{ and fail})$$
$$\qquad + P(\text{from } C \text{ and fail})$$
$$= P(A) \cdot P(F \mid A) + P(B) \cdot P(F \mid B) + P(C) \cdot P(F \mid C)$$
$$= (0.30 \times 0.02) + (0.45 \times 0.12) + (0.25 \times 0.04)$$
$$= 0.07$$

(b) P(from *A* | belt failed strength test $= \dfrac{P(A \cap F)}{P(F)}$

$$= \frac{(0.3 \times 0.02)}{0.07} = 0.0857$$

(c) Now we have the extra information that:
$P(A \text{ fails safety}) = 0.05$ independent of strength fail.
$P(B \text{ fails both strength and safety}) = 0.01$ (1%).
$P(C \text{ fails safety} \mid C \text{ fails strength}) = 0.5$.

So P(belt fails strength and safety)
$$= P(\text{belt from } A) \cdot P(F \mid A) \cdot P(\text{fails safety} \mid A)$$
$$\qquad + P(\text{belt from } B) \cdot P(\text{fails both} \mid B)$$
$$\qquad\qquad + P(\text{belt from } C) \cdot P(F \mid C) \cdot P(\text{fails safety} \mid C \text{ failed strength})$$
$$= (0.30 \times 0.02 \times 0.05) + (0.45 \times 0.01) + (0.25 \times 0.04 \times 0.5)$$
$$= 0.0098$$

Worked example 1.10

A market researcher wishes to interview residents aged 18 years and over in a small village. The age population of the village is made up as follows.

Age group	Male	Female
18–29	16	24
30–59	29	21
60 and over	15	25

(a) When one person is selected at random for interview;

A is the event of the person selected being male
B is the event of the person selected being in the age group 30–59
C is the event of the person selected being aged 60 or over.

(A′, B′, C′ are the events not A, not B and not C.)

Write down the value of:
(i) P(A),
(ii) P(A ∩ B),
(iii) P(A ∪ C′),
(iv) P(B′ | A).

(b) When three people are selected for interview, what is the probability that they are all female if:
(i) one is selected at random from each age group,
(ii) they are selected at random, without replacement, from the population of 130 people?

Three people are selected at random, without replacement.

(c) What is the probability that there will be one from each of the three age groups?

In the 18–29 age group, 45% own a bicycle, as do 30% in the 30–59 age group and 35% in the 60 and over age group.

(d) What is the probability that a person selected at random will
(i) own a bicycle,
(ii) be in the 30–59 age group, given that this person owns a bicycle?

Solution

(a) (i) $P(A) = \dfrac{60}{130} = \dfrac{6}{13}$,

(ii) $P(A \cap B) = P(\text{male aged between } 30\text{–}59) = \dfrac{29}{130}$,

(iii) $P(A \cup C') = P(\text{male, or } \mathbf{not} \text{ aged 60 or over, or both})$
$$= \frac{16 + 29 + 15 + 24 + 21}{130} = \frac{105}{130} = \frac{21}{26},$$

(iv) $P(B' \mid A) = P(\mathbf{not} \text{ in age 30–59 when known to be male})$
$$= \frac{16 + 15}{60} = \frac{31}{60}.$$

Always find totals first

Age	M	F	Total
18–29	16	24	40
30–59	29	21	50
60+	15	25	40
Total	60	70	130

(b) (i) P(female and one from each age group)

= P(one 18–29) . P(one 30–59) . P(one 60 or over)

$$= \frac{24}{40} \times \frac{21}{50} \times \frac{25}{40} = 0.1575,$$

(ii) P(female, selected from total 130 **without** replacement)

$$= \frac{70}{130} \times \frac{69}{129} \times \frac{68}{128} = 0.153007 = 0.153;$$

(c) P(three people, one from each age group, **without** replacement)

= 6 × P(one 18–29) . P(one 30–59) . P(one 60 or over)

$$= 6 \times \frac{40}{130} \times \frac{50}{129} \times \frac{40}{128} = 0.22361 = 0.224;$$

> Be careful that you remember to multiply by 6 as there are six different ways the three people can be chosen with one from each age group.

(d) Let D be the event 'owns a bicycle'

(i) P(D) = P(age 18–29) . P(D | age 18–29) +

P(age 30–59) . P(D | age 30–59) +

P(age 60 or over) . P(D | age 60 or over)

$$= \frac{40}{130} \times 0.45 + \frac{50}{130} \times 0.30 + \frac{40}{130} \times 0.35 = 0.36154$$

$$= 0.362,$$

> D is made up of three mutually exclusive events.

(ii) P(age 30–59 | D) = $\dfrac{\text{P(age 30–59 and have bicycle)}}{\text{P(D)}}$

$$= \frac{\dfrac{50}{130} \times 0.30}{0.36154} = 0.319.$$

> P(D) was found in **(d) (i)**.

EXERCISE 1C

1 Bottles are filled with tablets and checked for the correct number by a device which should 'bleep' when a bottle **not** containing the correct number of tablets is found. The device is faulty. The probability it gives a bleep when scanning a correctly filled bottle is 0.03. The probability it fails to bleep when scanning an incorrectly filled bottle is 0.04.

The probability a bottle is correctly filled is 0.95.

(a) Calculate the probability that the device emits a bleep when scanning a randomly chosen bottle;

(b) If the device emits a bleep, determine the probability that the randomly chosen bottle is incorrectly filled;

(c) Calculate the probability that the device responds correctly when scanning a randomly chosen bottle. [A]

2 Jackie attends college on Monday, Tuesday, Thursday and Friday each week. The probability of her being late on a particular day is shown in the table below and is independent of whether she was late on any previous day.

Day	Monday	Tuesday	Thursday	Friday
Probability late	0.4	0.2	0.2	0.3

What is the probability that during a particular week Jackie is:

(a) late every day,

(b) not late at all,

(c) late on exactly 1 day?

The probability that Jackie's friend Curtley is late is 0.1 if Jackie is not late and is 0.6 if Jackie is late.

What is the probability that on a particular Monday:

(d) both Jackie and Curtley are late,

(e) Curtley is late but Jackie is not,

(f) Curtley is late,

(g) Jackie is not late given that Curtley is late? [A]

3 A group of three pregnant women attend antenatal classes together. Assuming that each woman is equally likely to give birth on each of the 7 days in a week, find the probability that all three give birth

(a) on a Monday,

(b) on the same day of the week,

(c) on different days of the week,

(d) at a weekend (either a Saturday or Sunday).

(e) Find the probability of all three giving birth on the same day of the week given that they all give birth at a weekend. [A]

4 The staff employed by a college are classified as academic, administrative or support. The following table shows the numbers employed in these categories and their sex.

	Male	**Female**
Academic	42	28
Administrative	7	13
Support	26	9

A member of staff is selected at random.

A is the event that the person selected is female.
B is the event that the person selected is academic staff.
C is the event that the person selected is administrative staff.

(A' is the event not A, B' is the event not B, C' is the event not C.)

(a) Write down the values of:

    (i) $P(A)$,

    (ii) $P(A \cap B)$,

    (iii) $P(A \cup C')$,

    (iv) $P(A' \mid C)$.

(b) Write down one of the events which is:

    (i) not independent of A,

    (ii) independent of A,

    (iii) mutually exclusive of A.

In each case, justify your answer.

(c) Given that 90% of academic staff own cars, as do 80% of administrative staff and 30% of support staff:

    (i) What is the probability that a staff member selected at random owns a car?

    (ii) A staff member is selected at random and found to own a car. What is the probability that this person is a member of the support staff? [A]

5 A house is infested with mice and to combat this the householder acquired four cats. Albert, Belinda, Khalid and Poon. The householder observes that only half of the creatures caught are mice. A fifth are voles and the rest are birds.

20% of the catches are made by Albert, 45% by Belinda, 10% by Khalid and 25% by Poon.

(a) The probability of a catch being a mouse, a bird or a vole is independent of whether or not it is made by Albert. What is the probability of a randomly selected catch being:

    (i) a mouse caught by Albert,

    (ii) a bird not caught by Albert?

(b) Belinda's catches are equally likely to be a mouse, a bird or a vole. What is the probability of a randomly selected catch being a mouse caught by Belinda?

(c) The probability of a randomly selected catch being a mouse caught by Khalid is 0.05. What is the probability that a catch made by Khalid is a mouse?

(d) Given that the probability that a randomly selected catch is a mouse caught by Poon is 0.2 verify that the probability of a randomly selected catch being a mouse is 0.5.

(e) What is the probability that a catch which is a mouse was made by Belinda? [A]

6 Last year the employees of a firm either received no pay rise, a small pay rise or a large pay rise. The following table shows the number in each category, classified by whether they were weekly paid or monthly paid.

	No pay rise	Small pay rise	Large pay rise
Weekly paid	25	85	5
Monthly paid	4	8	23

A tax inspector decides to investigate the tax affairs of an employee selected at random.

D is the event that a weekly paid employee is selected.
E is the event that an employee who received no pay rise is selected.
D′ and E′ are the events 'not D' and 'not E' respectively.
Find:

(a) $P(D)$;   **(b)** $P(D \cup E)$;   **(c)** $P(D' \cap E')$;

F is the event that an employee is female.

(d) Given that $P(F') = 0.8$, find the number of female employees;

(e) Interpret $P(D \mid F)$ in the context of this question;

(f) Given that $P(D \cap F) = 0.1$, find $P(D \mid F)$.   [A]

7 Each week a statistics teacher gives out worksheets containing a large number of questions. Two students Zafar and Angie, sometimes work on the questions alone and sometimes work together. They find that if they work on a question together the probability of obtaining the correct answer is 0.9. If they work alone the probability that Zafar will obtain the correct answer is 0.7 and the probability that Angie will obtain the correct answer is 0.6.

(a) Zafar works alone on one question, Angie works alone on a second question and they work together on a third question. Find the probability that they obtain the correct answers to all three questions;

(b) If they work together on three questions, find the probability that they obtain exactly two correct answers.

A particular worksheet contains 25 questions. The two students use a random process to divide these questions into nine to be worked on alone by Zafar, six to be worked on alone by Angie and ten to be worked on together.

(c) Find the probability that a particular question, selected at random from this worksheet is:
   (i) worked on alone by Angie and answered correctly,
   (ii) answered correctly,
   (iii) worked on alone by Angie, given that it is answered correctly.   [A]

*8 The owner of a number of national newspapers bids to buy a famous football club. A large number of the club's supporters write letters to the editors of these newspapers. Of the letters, 90% are against the bid, 4% are neutral and 6% are in favour of the bid.

(a) If three letters are selected at random, find the probability that:
  (i) they will all be against the bid,
  (ii) one will be against the bid, one will be neutral and one will be in favour of the bid.

The probability that a letter is published is:

　　　0.01 if it is against the bid,
　　　0.24 if it is neutral,
　　　0.55 if it is in favour of the bid.

(b) Find the probability that a randomly selected letter is:
  (i) against the bid and is published,
  (ii) published,
  (iii) against the bid, given that it is published,
  (iv) against the bid, given that it is **not** published.   [A]

*9 The probability that telephone calls to a railway timetable enquiry service are answered is 0.7.

(a) If three calls are made, find the probability that:
  (i) all three are answered,
  (ii) exactly two are answered.

(b) Ahmed requires some timetable information and decides that if his call is not answered he will call repeatedly until he obtains an answer.

  Find the probability that to obtain an answer he has to call:
  (i) exactly three times,
  (ii) at least three times.

(c) If a call is answered, the probability that the information given is correct is 0.8. Thus, there are three possible outcomes for each call:

　　　call not answered,
　　　call answered but incorrect information given,
　　　call answered and correct information given.

  If three calls are made, find the probability that each outcome occurs once.

Two thousand calls are made to the enquiry service.

　　　B denotes the event that more than 1500 are answered.
　　　C denotes the event that exactly 1500 are answered.
　　　D denotes the event that less than 1500 are answered.
　　　E denotes the event that less than 1700 are answered.

(d) (i) Describe the event which is complementary to B.

Of the events B, C, D and E, write down:

(ii) two which are exhaustive but not mutually exclusive,

(iii) two which are neither exhaustive nor mutually exclusive,

(iv) three which are exhaustive and mutually exclusive.

[A]

10 During an epidemic of a certain disease a doctor is consulted by 110 people suffering from symptoms commonly associated with the disease. Of the 110 people, 45 are female of whom 20 actually have the disease and 25 do not. Fifteen males have the disease and the rest do not.

(a) A person is selected at random. The event that this person is female is denoted by A and the event that this person is suffering from the disease is denoted by B. Evaluate

(i) P(A),

(ii) $P(A \cup B)$,

(iii) $P(A \cap B)$,

(iv) $P(A \mid B)$.

(b) If three different people are selected at random without replacement what is the probability of

(i) all three having the disease,

(ii) exactly one of the three having the disease,

(iii) one of the three being a female with the disease, one a male with the disease and one a female without the disease?

(c) Of people with the disease 96% react positively to a test for diagnosing the disease as do 8% of people without the disease. What is the probability of a person selected at random

(i) reacting positively,

(ii) having the disease given that he or she reacted positively? [A]

11 Three friends *A*, *B* and *C* share a flat. The probability of an incoming telephone call in the evening being for *A*, *B* or *C* is 0.2, 0.3 and 0.5 respectively. The probability that *A* is at home when it is received is 0.75. The corresponding probabilities for *B* and *C* are 0.5 and 0.8 respectively. All the probabilities are independent.

Find the probability that for an incoming call in the evening

(a) no one is at home to answer the telephone;

(b) the call is for *A* and *A* is at home;

(c) the person to whom the call is made is at home;

(d) the call is for *A*, given that the person to whom the call is made is at home;

(e) the call is for *A*, and *A* is the only one of the three not at home. [A]

Key point summary

1 The **union** of two events A and B is denoted A ∪ B,   *p1*
the event that 'A or B or both occur'.
The **intersection** of two events A and B is denoted
A ∩ B, the event that 'both A and B occur'.

2 The probability of the event A ∪ B is given by: *p1*

$$P(A \cup B) = P(A) + P(B) - P(A \cap B)$$

3 For **independent** events, the probability of A ∩ B   *p6*
is given by:

$$P(A \cap B) = P(A) \cdot P(B)$$

This is the **multiplication** law

4 P(A | B) denotes the **conditional** probability that   *p9*
event A occurs **given** the information that B occurs
or has occurred.

5 The probability of the intersection of two events   *p9*
A and B can also be found from:

$$P(A \cap B) = P(A) \cdot P(B \mid A)$$

or

$$= P(B) \cdot P(A \mid B)$$

6 For **independent** events A and B: *p9*

$$P(A \mid B) = P(A)$$

and

$$P(B \mid A) = P(B)$$

7 As an example, for three separate mutually exclusive   *p11*
and exhaustive events B_1, B_2 and B_3 the **total
probability theorem** tell us that:

$$P(A) = P(B_1) \cdot P(A \mid B_1)$$
$$+ P(B_2).P(A \mid B_2)$$
$$+ P(B_3).P(A \mid B_3)$$

There may be only two such mutually exclusive events
involved. It is most unlikely that you would encounter
more than three events in S3.

8 The simplified version of Bayes' Theorem which will be   *p12*
required for evaluation of conditional probabilities is:

$$P(B \mid A) = \frac{P(A \cap B)}{P(A)}$$

where P(A) is usually obtained using the total
probability theorem.

Test yourself	**What to review**
1 For two events A and B, explain the meaning of the conditional events **(a)** A | B; **(b)** B | A.	*Section 1.3*
2 If , for two independent events A and B, P(A) = 0.6 and P(B) = 0.7 find the probabilities: **(a)** P(A ∩ B); **(b)** P(A ∪ B).	*Section 1.1*
3 Information is supplied on a group of young adult drivers concerning whether or not they had been involved in a road accident in the last 12 months.	*Sections 1.1 and 1.2*

	Accident	**No accident**
Male	2	38
Female	3	57

For a driver randomly selected from this group, find the probability that:

(a) the driver is male;

(b) the driver has not had an accident;

(c) the driver is male and has had an accident;

(d) the driver has had an accident given that it is known the driver is male.

Are the events 'driver is male' and 'driver has had an accident' independent events ?

4 At a school, it is known that 60% of pupils live over 3 miles away. Of these pupils, 90% never walk or ride a bicycle to school. Of the pupils who live 3 miles or less away, it is known that 70% do sometimes walk or ride a bicycle to school.	*Section 1.4*

Find the probability that a randomly selected pupil

(a) lives over 3 miles away from school and sometimes walks or rides a bike to school;

(b) sometimes walks or rides a bike to school.

5 In a factory three machines *1*, *2* and *3* are used to produce a particular component. It is known that machine *1* produces 10%, machine *2* produces 40% and machine *3* produces 50% of these components.	*Section 1.4*

The percentage of imperfect components from machine *1* is 2%, from machine *2* is 5% and from machine *3* is 4%.

Find the probability that a component, chosen at random from this production process, is imperfect.

Test yourself (continued)

What to review

6 A test for a disease PKU is carried out on all newborn babies. This test has a probability of 0.05 of registering a positive result for babies who do not have PKU and a probability of 0.04 of registering a negative result for babies who do have PKU.

Sections 1.4 and 1.5

It is known that around 1% of babies have PKU.

If R is the event 'baby has PKU'
S is the event 'positive result'
T is the event 'negative result'

Find the values of

(a) P(R);

(b) P(S | R);

(c) P(T).

(d) P(R | T).

Test yourself ANSWERS

1 (a) A occurs given you know B has occurred;

(b) B occurs given you know A has occurred.

2 (a) $0.6 \times 0.7 = 0.42$; **(b)** $0.6 + 0.7 - 0.42 = 0.88$.

3 (a) 0.4; **(b)** 0.95;

(c) 0.02; **(d)** 0.05, P(A | M) = 0.05 = P(A), yes.

4 (a) $0.6 \times 0.10 = 0.06$; **(b)** $(0.6 \times 0.10) + (0.4 \times 0.7) = 0.34$.

5 $(0.1 \times 0.02) + (0.4 \times 0.05) + (0.5 \times 0.04) = 0.042$.

6 (a) 0.01; **(b)** 0.96;

(c) $(0.99 \times 0.95) + (0.01 \times 0.04) = 0.9409 = P(T)$;

(d) $\left(\dfrac{0.01 \times 0.04}{0.9409} = 0.0000425 \right)$.

CHAPTER 2

Hypothesis testing

Learning objectives

After studying this chapter you should be able to:

■ define a null and an alternative hypothesis
■ define the significance level of a hypothesis test
■ identify a critical region
■ understand when to use a one- or two-tailed test
■ understand what is meant by a Type 1 and a Type 2 error
■ carry out a hypothesis test concerning a product moment correlation coefficient.

2.1 Forming a hypothesis

One of the most important applications of statistics is to use a **sample** to test an idea, or **hypothesis**, you have regarding a population. This branch of statistics is known as **inferential** statistics.

Conclusions can never be absolutely certain but the risk of your conclusion being incorrect can be quantified (measured) and can enable you to identify **statistically significant** results.

> Statistically significant results require overwhelming evidence.

In any experiment, you will have your own idea or hypothesis as to how you expect the results to turn out.

A **null hypothesis**, written H_0, is set up at the start of any hypothesis test. This null hypothesis is a statement which defines the population and so always contains '=' signs, never '>', '<' or '≠'.

> The **null hypothesis** is only abandoned in the face of overwhelming evidence that it cannot explain the experimental results. In a court of law, defendants are considered innocent until the evidence proves their guilt beyond reasonable doubt. Similarly, H_0 is accepted as true until results are obtained which suggest, overwhelmingly, that it is not true.

Examples of null hypotheses are:
H_0 Population median $= 500$ hours
H_0 Population product moment correlation coefficient (PMCC), $\rho = 0$.

Usually, you are hoping to show that the null hypothesis is not true and so the **alternative hypothesis**, written H_1, is often the hypothesis you want to establish. Examples are:
H_1 Population median > 500 hours
H_1 Population PMCC, $\rho \neq 0$
H_1 Population PMCC, $\rho < 0$.

> It often seems strange to students that they may want to show that H_0 is **not** true but, considering the examples of H_0 and H_1 given here, a manufacturer may well hope to show that bulbs now have a **longer** average lifetime than the previously quoted 500 hours.

> A hypothesis test needs two hypotheses identified at the beginning:
>
> H_0 the **null hypothesis** and
> H_1 the **alternative hypothesis**.

> H_0 states that a situation is unchanged, that a population parameter takes its usual value.
>
> H_1 states that the parameter has increased, decreased or just changed.

2.2 One- and two-tailed tests

Tests which involve an H_1 with a $>$ or $<$ sign are called **one-tailed** tests because you expect to find just an increase or just a decrease.

Tests which involve an H_1 with a $\neq$ sign are called **two-tailed** tests as they consider any change (whether it be an increase or decrease).

For example, if data were collected on the amount of weekly pocket money given to a random selection of children aged between 12 and 14 in a rural area, and also in a city, it may be that you are interested in investigating whether children in the city are given **more** pocket money than children in rural areas. Therefore, you may set up your hypotheses as:

H_0 Average pocket money of children is the same in the rural area and in the city, or
Population median (city) = Population median (rural)
H_1 Average pocket money **greater** in city, or
Population median (city) > Population median (rural).

This is an example of a **one-tailed** test.

However, if you were monitoring the weight of items produced in a factory, it would be likely that **any** change, be it an increase or decrease, would be a problem and there would not necessarily be any reason to expect a change of a specific type.
In this case, typical hypotheses would be:

H_0 Population mean weight is 35g

$$\mu = 35g$$

H_1 Population mean weight **is not** 35g

$$\mu \neq 35g$$

This is an example of a **two-tailed** test.

One-tailed tests will generally involve words such as:
• better or worse
• faster or slower
• more or less
• bigger or smaller
• increase or decrease
or inverse/direct for correlation coefficients.

In the example here,
H_1 Population median > 500 hours indicates a **one-tailed** test.

Two-tailed tests will generally involve words such as:
• different or difference
• change
• affected.

> A **two-tailed test** involves testing for any (non-directional) change in a parameter.
>
> A **one-tailed test** involves testing for a specific increase or decrease (change in one direction only).

2.3 Testing a hypothesis about a product moment correlation coefficient

In S1, the concept of correlation was introduced and the method for evaluating a product moment correlation coefficient (PMCC) was given. Interpretation of a value for a sample PMCC was restricted to comments of the type 'very high positive correlation is evident' or 'slight negative correlation is evident'.

Carrying out a hypothesis test to determine whether a population PMCC, ρ, is **significantly** different from zero is very simple and involves a **test statistic** which is the sample PMCC, r, and its comparison with a **critical value** to be found in Table 8 of the formulae book.

> The **parameter**, ρ, is the population PMCC about which you will come to a conclusion after consideration of the sample **statistic**, r.

The simplest way to explain the procedure to follow when carrying out a hypothesis test on a population PMCC is to work through an example.

Consider the following data gathered on fuel consumption and speed:

Speed X (km per hour)	85	102	38	42	135	75	51
Fuel consumption Y (km per litre)	6.9	7.3	11.1	10.1	6.1	8.3	8.6

> If a different sample was chosen, a different value of r would have been obtained, but ρ, the population PMCC, remains constant.
>
> If $\rho = 0$, r is very unlikely to be exactly 0 but it is likely to be fairly close to 0.

The PMCC for this sample data, $r = -0.913$, is found directly from a calculator.
The obvious comment is that there is very strong evidence to suggest an inverse linear relationship between speed and fuel consumption.
To test this formally, the null and alternative hypotheses $\mathbf{H_0}$ and $\mathbf{H_1}$ must be stated at the start of the testing procedure.

$\qquad$ $\mathbf{H_0}\ \rho = 0$

(**No** significant correlation exists in population between speed and fuel consumption.)

$\qquad$ $\mathbf{H_1}\ \rho < 0$

(Population correlation coefficient is significantly less than zero since we expect less km per litre at higher speeds.)

> Note that, in this test, the null hypothesis is that there is **no** correlation and this must be rejected for you to conclude that significant correlation exists in the population.

This is a **one-tailed** test and we will use the standard **significance level** of 5%.

> The test is **one-tailed** because the H_1 involves $<$, that is ρ **less** than zero.

The **test statistic**, $r = -0.913$, has been calculated from the sample of seven pairs, $n = 7$.

> The **significance level** is the level of overwhelming evidence deemed necessary for the decision to conclude H_0 is **not** true.

The **critical value** relevant for this test is found from Table 8 by reading along the row where $n = 7$ and selecting the column which gives values for a one-tailed test at 5% significance level.

For these data, the **critical value** is -0.6694.

> In this case, H_0 is accepted if r is close to zero or above zero. The critical value defines what is meant by 'close to'.

Note that the critical values given are all positive. The nature of the test being carried out will determine if a negative critical value is relevant.

The H_1 indicates that we must consider extreme values for $\rho < 0$, that is extreme negative values.

The **test statistic** $r = -0.913$ is now compared with -0.6694.

> If $r < -0.6694$ then H_0 is rejected. The test is **one-tailed**.

If $r > -0.6694$, then we **accept** H_0 and conclude that there is **no significant** evidence that there is an inverse correlation between speed and consumption.

If, as in this case, $r \leqslant -0.6694$ we **reject** H_0 and conclude that there is **significant** evidence of correlation between speed and fuel consumption in the population.

> The range of possible values for r which are equal to or less than the critical value is known as the **critical region**.
>
>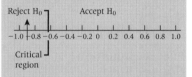
>
> If a sample PMCC test statistic lies in the critical region, then H_0 is rejected. If it does not lie in the critical region, then H_0 is accepted.

The conclusion made is that the sample PMCC, $r = -0.913$, offers significant evidence, at the 5% level, of the existence of inverse correlation between speed and fuel consumption.

There is a linear relationship between the speed and the fuel consumption in the population such that as speed increases, fuel consumption decreases.

> Conclusions should not just be given in general terms but should always refer to the specific data involved in the test.

The **critical values** given in Table 8 assume that the data comes from a **bivariate normal** distribution. Discussion of this distribution is beyond the scope of S3.

Generally, it is safe to use these critical values unless some features of the data – such as an extreme outlier – suggests otherwise.

Note that the **critical values** given in Table 8 are for **one-tailed** or for **two-tailed** tests and care must be taken to ensure the correct **critical value** is used depending on the nature of the test concerned.

Example 2.1 involves another **one-tailed** test and Example 2.2 involves a two-tailed test.

> The **critical region** or **critical value** identifies the range of extreme values which lead to the rejection of H_0.

Worked example 2.1

A group of antiques collectors is invited to estimate the likely price to be made at auction for a selection of eight different items. Their estimates, together with the actual prices achieved at auction, are given below.

Item	A	B	C	D	E	F	G	H
Price estimate	£350	£125	£75	£100	£25	£550	£750	£15
Actual price	£270	£140	£68	£85	£34	£390	£820	£18

Calculate the product moment correlation coefficient between the estimates made by the group of collectors and the actual prices achieved at auction.

Comment on the value of this correlation coefficient.

Stating clearly your null and alternative hypotheses, investigate whether there is a direct correlation between the estimated and actual prices. Use a 5% significance level.

> The question suggests that a direct correlation is to be tested for and so a **one-tailed** test is relevant.

Solution

The PMCC for this sample data, $r = 0.967$ is found directly from a calculator.

The **test statistic** $r = 0.967$.
The clear comment is that there is very strong evidence to suggest a direct correlation between estimated and actual price. To test this formally, the null and alternative hypotheses H_0 and H_1 are stated.

H_0 $\rho = 0$

(**No** significant correlation exists in population between estimated and actual price.)

H_1 $\rho > 0$

(Population correlation coefficient is significantly greater than zero.)

This is a **one-tailed** test with **significance level** of 5%.

The **test statistic**, $r = 0.967$, has been calculated from the sample of eight pairs, $n = 8$.

The **critical value** is found from Table 8 where $n = 8$ for a one-tailed test at 5%. The **critical value** = 0.6215.

In this case, $r > 0.6215$ and so there is significant evidence to reject $\mathbf{H_0}$ and conclude that there is a strong direct correlation between estimated and actual prices.

> If $r \geqslant 0.6215$ then $\mathbf{H_0}$ is rejected. The test is **one-tailed**.
>
>
> Remember that if r is **less** than the **critical value** for this one-tailed test, we accept $\mathbf{H_0}$ and conclude that there is no significant evidence of a correlation between prices.

Worked example 2.2

The results given show the yield y, in grams from a chemical experiment corresponding to an input of x grams of a certain chemical to the process.

Input x gram	5.6	6.3	8.5	4.2	7.4	5.1	9.6	4.8	6.9	5.9
Yield y gram	82	78	86	65	91	80	75	72	89	74

Calculate the product moment correlation coefficient between the input and the yield.
Comment on the value of this correlation coefficient.
Stating clearly your null and alternative hypotheses, investigate whether there is an association between the input and the yield. Use a 5% significance level.

> There is no suggestion that a direct or an inverse correlation is to be tested for and so a **two-tailed** test is relevant.

Solution

The PMCC for this sample data, $r = 0.484$ is found directly from a calculator.
The **test statistic,** $r = 0.484$.

This value for r indicates a slight, direct correlation between input and yield.

To test the significance of this result, the hypotheses are:

$$\mathbf{H_0}\ \rho = 0$$

(**No** significant correlation exists in population between input and yield.)

$$\mathbf{H_1}\ \rho \neq 0$$

(Population correlation coefficient is significantly different from zero.)

This is a **two-tailed** test with **significance level** of 5%.

The **test statistic**, $r = 0.484$ has been calculated from the sample of ten pairs, $n = 10$.

The **critical value** is found from Table 8 where $n = 10$ for a two-tailed test at 5%. The **critical value** $= 0.6319$.

In this case, $|r| < 0.6319$ and so there is no significant evidence to doubt H_0.

We accept H_0 and conclude that there is no significant evidence to indicate a correlation between input and yield in the population.

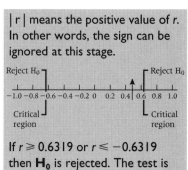

$|r|$ means the positive value of r. In other words, the sign can be ignored at this stage.

If $r \geqslant 0.6319$ or $r \leqslant -0.6319$ then H_0 is rejected. The test is two-tailed.

EXERCISE 2A

1 A scientist, working in an agricultural research station, believes there is a relationship between the hardness of shells laid by chickens and the amount of a food supplement put into the diet of the chickens. He selects ten chickens of the same breed and gains the following results:

(a) Calculate the product moment correlation coefficient between the level of supplement and the hardness of shell;

(b) Stating clearly your null and alternative hypotheses, investigate whether there is an association between level of supplement and shell hardness. Use a 5% significance level for this two-tailed test.

Chicken	Level of food supplement x (g)	Shell hardness y
A	7.0	1.2
B	9.8	2.1
C	11.6	3.4
D	17.5	6.1
E	7.6	1.3
F	8.2	1.7
G	12.4	3.4
H	17.5	6.2
I	9.5	2.1
J	19.5	7.1

2 The body and heart mass of 14 10-month-old male mice are given below.

(a) Calculate the value of the product moment correlation coefficient for this data;

(b) Stating clearly your null and alternative hypotheses, test using a 5% significance level, whether there is a direct association between body mass and heart mass. This is a one-tailed test.

Body mass x (g)	Heart mass y (mg)
27	118
30	136
37	156
38	150
32	140
36	155
32	157
32	114
38	144
42	159
36	149
44	170
33	131
38	160

3 The following table gives the inflation rate x and the unemployment rate y for ten different countries during December 1979.

Country	Inflation rate x (%)	Unemployment rate y (%)
A	13.9	2.9
B	21.4	11.3
C	9.6	5.4
D	1.5	6.1
E	31.7	9.0
F	23.1	8.8
G	18.4	5.9
H	34.4	15.6
I	27.6	9.8
J	5.6	3.7

(a) Calculate the value of the product moment correlation coefficient between inflation and unemployment rates;

(b) Test, using a 5% significance level, the hypothesis $\mathbf{H_0}\,\rho = 0$ against the alternative hypothesis $\mathbf{H_1}\,\rho \neq 0$, where ρ is the population correlation coefficient between the rates.

4 In a workshop producing hand-made goods a score is assigned to each finished item on the basis of its quality (the better the quality the higher the score). The number of items produced by each of the 15 craftsmen on a particular day and their average quality score are given in the following table.

Craftsman	Items produced x	Average quality y
1	14	6.2
2	23	7.3
3	17	4.9
4	32	7.1
5	16	5.2
6	19	5.7
7	17	5.9
8	25	6.4
9	27	7.3
10	31	6.1
11	17	5.4
12	18	5.7
13	26	6.9
14	24	7.2
15	22	4.8

(a) Calculate the product moment correlation coefficient between number produced and quality score;

(b) Using a 5% significance level, test whether there is any evidence of an association between number produced and average quality score. State clearly your null and alternative hypotheses.

*5 A hospital doctor was interested in the percentage of a certain drug absorbed by patients. She obtained the following data on 10 patients taking the drug on two separate days.

			Percentage of drug absorbed			
Patient		1	2	3	4	5
Day 1	x	35.5	16.6	13.6	42.5	28.5
Day 2	y	27.6	15.1	12.9	34.1	35.5
Patient		6	7	8	9	10
Day 1	x	30.3	8.7	21.5	16.4	32.3
Day 2	y	32.5	84.3	21.5	11.1	36.4

(a) Draw a scatter diagram of the data;

(b) Calculate the product moment correlation coefficient between the percentage of drug absorbed on Day 1 and Day 2;

(c) Stating clearly your null and alternative hypotheses, investigate whether there is an association between drug absorption on Day 1 and Day 2. Use a 5% significance level;

(d) After examining the scatter diagram, the doctor found that one of the points was surprising. Further checking revealed this point was the result of abnormal circumstances. The value of the product moment correlation coefficient for the remaining 9 points is 0.863.

  (i) State which point has been omitted.

  (ii) Test again, using a 5% significance level, whether there is an association between the drug absorption on the 2 days. [A]

6 The following table shows the latitude, maximum and minimum temperature for 15 towns in a particular year.

Town	Latitude	Maximum temperature (°C)	Maximum temperature (°C)
A	60	8	0
B	53	14	6
C	52	14	9
D	44	18	6
E	60	10	2
F	45	17	8
G	50	12	6
H	60	8	1
I	39	20	14
J	56	11	5
K	40	22	11
L	53	13	4
M	49	16	7
N	52	12	10
O	42	25	12

(a) Calculate the product moment correlation coefficient between mid-temperature (mid-way between maximum and minimum temperature) and latitude;

(b) Investigate, using a 1% significance level, whether mid-temperature is associated with latitude. [A]

2.4 Significance levels and problems to consider

You may well already have wondered why the **significance level** used in hypothesis testing is commonly set at 5%. Other significance levels which are sometimes used are 10%, 1% and 0.1%.

A common question asked by students is:
Why is the level of overwhelming evidence necessary to lead to rejection of H_0 commonly set at 5%?

The **significance level** of a hypothesis test gives the

P(test statistic lies inside critical region | H_0 true)

In other words, *if* the H_0 is true, then you would expect a result as extreme as this only once in every 20 times with a 5% significance level. The result is *statistically significant* with this level of extreme result and the H_0 is deemed **not** to be true.

Sometimes it may be necessary to be 'more certain' of a conclusion. If a traditional trusted piece of research is to be challenged, then a 1% level of significance may be used to ensure greater confidence in rejecting the H_0.
If a new drug is to be used in preference to a well-known one then a 0.1% level may be necessary to ensure that no chance or fluke effects occur in research which leads to conclusions which may affect human health.

The **significance level** of a test is the probability that a test statistic lies in the extreme critical region, on the assumption H_0 is true. It determines the level of overwhelming evidence deemed necessary for the rejection of H_0.

The general procedure for hypothesis is as follows:
1 Write down H_0 and H_1.
2 Decide which test to use.
3 Decide on the significance level.
4 Identify the critical region.
5 Calculate the test statistic.
6 Make your conclusion.

2.5 Errors

It is often quite a surprising concept for students to realise that, having correctly carried out a hypothesis test on carefully collected data and having made the relevant conclusion to accept the H_0 as true or to reject it as false, this conclusion might be right or it might be wrong.

However, you can never be absolutely certain that your conclusion is correct and not the result of a *freak* result. The significance level identifies for you the risk of a freak result leading to a wrong decision to reject H_0.

This leads many students to ask why tests so often use a **5% significance level** which has a probability of 0.05 of incorrectly rejecting H_0 when it actually is true. Why not reduce the significance level to 0.1% and then there would be a negligible chance of 0.001 of this error occurring?

The answer to this question comes from considering the **two** errors which may occur when conducting a hypothesis test. This table illustrates the problems:

		Conclusion made	
		H_0 true	H_0 not true
Reality	H_0 correct	Conclusion correct	Error made **Type 1**
	H_0 incorrect	Error made **Type 2**	Conclusion correct

Not only can you conclude H_0 is true when really it is false but also you could conclude it is false when actually it is true.

This table shows that the **significance level** of a test is:

P(conclusion H_0 not true | H_0 really is correct)
   = P(**Type 1** error made)

The other error to consider is when a statistician does not achieve a significant, extreme result even though the H_0 actually is **not** true.

P(conclusion H_0 true | H_0 really is incorrect)
   = P(**Type 2** error made)

The probability of making a Type 2 error is difficult or impossible to evaluate unless precise further information is available about values of parameters within the population. If a value suggested in H_0 is only slightly incorrect then there may be a very high probability of making a Type 2 error. If the value is completely incorrect then the probability of a Type 2 error will be very small.

You will not be expected to evaluate the probability of making a Type 2 error in S3.

Obviously, if you set a very low **significance level** for a test, then the probability of making a Type 1 error will be low but you may well have quite a high probability of making a Type 2 error.

There is no logical reason why 5% is used, rather than 4% or 6%. However, practical experience over a long period of time has shown that, in most circumstances, a significance level of 5% gives a good balance between the risks of making Type 1 and Type 2 errors. This is why 5% is chosen as the 'standard' significance level for hypothesis testing and careful considerations must be made to change this value.

> If you set a very low probability for risking rejection of H_0 then you are unlikely to obtain the most extreme result from the sample that would lead you to reject it, unless H_0 was suggesting a situation that was 'miles away' from reality.

Errors which can occur are as follows.
A Type 1 error which is to reject H_0 when it actually is true.
A Type 2 error which is to accept H_0 when it is actually not true.

Worked example 2.3

Two sets of times, measured in 1/100ths of a second, were obtained from nine subjects who were involved in two similar psychology experiments.
The product moment correlation coefficient for these nine pairs was found to be 0.879.
The hypothesis that there is no correlation between the results of the two experiments is to be tested using a 1% level of significance.

(a) Explain, in this context, what is meant by a Type 1 error;

(b) Explain, in this context, what is meant by a Type 2 error;

(c) Carry out the test.

Solution

(a) A Type 1 error is to conclude that there is a significant correlation between the results of the two experiments when, in reality, there is no significant correlation between the results in the population;

(b) A Type 2 error is to conclude that there is no correlation between the experimental results when, in reality, there is a significant correlation between the experimental results in the population;

(c) H_0 $\rho = 0$
H_1 $\rho \neq 0$
The **critical value** for a two-sided 1% **significance level** with nine pairs of points is 0.7977.
Since the **test statistic** is 0.879 H_0 is rejected and we conclude, at the 1% significance level, that there is direct correlation between the experimental results in the population.

EXERCISE 2B

1 Refer to Question **1** in Exercise 2A and explain, in the context of this question, the meaning of a Type 1 error.

2 Refer to Question **2** in Exercise 2A and explain, in the context of this question, the meaning of a Type 2 error.

3 A local authority offers all its employees regular health checks. As part of the check, several physiological measurements are taken on each person. The results for two of the measurements X and Y on nine people are shown.

Person	X	Y
1	9	10
2	31	21
3	29	31
4	50	15
5	54	34
6	69	44
7	76	61
8	91	51
9	95	64

(a) Draw a scatter diagram of this data;

(b) Calculate the product moment correlation coefficient between the two measurements;

(c) Stating the null and alternative hypotheses used, test whether there is a direct association between the two measurements. The significance level is 5%.

(d) Explain in the context of this question the meaning of a Type 1 and a Type 2 error.

4 During the lambing season, eight ewes and their lambs were weighed at the time of birth with the following results:

Ewe	Weight of ewe x (kg)	Weight of lamb y (kg)
A	44	3.5
B	41	2.8
C	43	3.2
D	40	2.7
E	41	2.9
F	37	2.5
G	38	2.8
H	35	2.6

(a) Calculate the product moment correlation coefficient between weight of ewe and weight of lamb;

(b) Test whether these data could have come from a population with correlation coefficient $\rho = 0$.
Use a 1% significance level;

(c) Explain in the context of this question, the meaning of a Type 1 and a Type 2 error.

*5 The following data is from the 1971 census, Northumberland County Report, Part III.

District	Population x (hundreds)	No. with no access to hot water supply y	No. in households with exclusive use flush toilets z (hundreds)
Bedlingtonshire	281	1225	240
Berwick	113	300	109
Blyth	343	1645	277
Gosforth	256	260	237
Hexham	92	160	81
Longbenton	486	680	454
Morpeth	128	145	120
Newbiggin	106	120	93
Newburn	392	795	359
Prudhoe	96	140	86
Seaton	318	620	284

Calculate the product moment correlation coefficient between:

(a) x and y;

(b) x and z;

(c) y and z;

(d) Stating the null and alternative hypotheses used, test, at a 5% significance level, whether there is an association between x and y, x and z or y and z;

(e) Discuss your results further in the light of the following comment from a housing expert: 'I would expect areas with a large number of people with no access to hot water supply to have a small number of people with exclusive use of inside flush toilets.' [A]

6 As part of an educational study, a random sample of ten boys from Harrowing School was given, after suitable preparation, three tests. These were an IQ test, a written test in Latin and a practical test in Music. Each boy was given a mark out of 100 on each test and these results are summarised in the following table:

Boy	Latin score (y)	IQ score (x)	Music score (z)
A	58	73	78
B	67	84	50
C	41	55	45
D	59	69	42
E	61	75	58
F	45	52	35
G	78	79	55
H	53	72	52
I	50	65	38
J	85	89	62

2

(a) Calculate the product moment correlation coefficient between:

    (i)   IQ score and Latin score;

    (ii)   IQ score and Music score;

(b) Stating the null and alternative hypotheses, test, at the 5% level of significance, whether there is a direct association between IQ and Latin scores or between IQ and Music scores;

(c) Would your answers to part (b) be affected if the tests had been carried out at the 1% significance level?   [A]

*7 A tasting panel was asked to assess biscuits baked from a new recipe. Each member of the panel was asked to assign a score on a scale from 0 to 100 for texture (X_1), flavour (X_2), sweetness(X_3), chewiness (X_4) and butteriness (X_5).

The scores assigned by the ten members of the panel for texture and flavour were as follows:

Taster	1	2	3	4	5	6	7	8	9	10
X_1	43	59	76	28	53	55	81	49	38	47
X_2	67	82	75	48	91	63	67	51	44	54

(a) Draw a scatter diagram of the data;

(b) Calculate the product moment correlation coefficient between X_1 and X_2;

(c) State briefly, how you would expect the scatter diagram in (a) to alter if the tasters were given training in how to assign scores before the tasting took place;

(d) The product moment correlation coefficient between flavour (X_2) and sweetness (X_3) is 0.858, carry out a test, using a 5% significance level, to determine whether a direct association exists between flavour and sweetness;

(e) The table below shows the product moment correlation coefficient between each pair of X_1, X_2, X_3 and X_4. Complete this table.

	X_1	X_2	X_3	X_4
X_1	1		0.232	−0.989
X_2		1		−0.478
X_3			1	−0.251
X_4				1

If a decision was made that to save time in future only X_1, X_2 and either X_3 or X_4 would be recorded which variable (X_3 or X_4) would you omit and why?

(f) Given that the correlation coefficient between X_2 and X_5 is exactly 1 what is the correlation between X_3 and X_5?   [A]

*8 (a) The product moment correlation coefficient between the random variables W and X is 0.71 and between the random variables Y and Z is -0.05.

For each of these pairs of variables sketch a scatter diagram which might represent the results which gave the correlation coefficients;

(b) The scatter diagram below shows the amounts of the pollutants nitrogen oxides and carbon monoxide emitted by the exhausts of 46 vehicles. Both variables are measured in grams of the pollutant per mile driven.

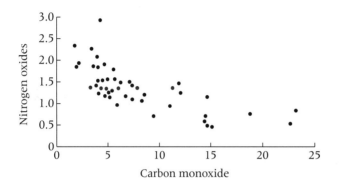

Write down three noticeable features of this scatter diagram.

It has been suggested that 'If an engine is out of tune, it emits more of all the important pollutants. You can find out how badly a vehicle is polluting the air by measuring any one pollutant. If that value is acceptable, the other emissions will also be acceptable'.

State, giving your reason, whether or not this scatter diagram supports the above suggestion;

(c) When investigating the amount of heat evolved during the hardening of cement a scientist monitored the amount of heat evolved Y, in calories/g of cement, and four explanatory variables X_1, X_2, X_3 and X_4. Based on 13 observations the scientist produced the following correlation matrix.

	Y	X_1	X_2	X_3	X_4
Y	1	0.731	0.816	-0.535	-0.821
X_1		1	0.229	r	-0.245
X_2			1	-0.139	-0.973
X_3				1	0.030
X_4					1

The values of X_1 and X_3 are as follows:

X_1	7	1	11	11	7	11	3	1	2	21	1	11	10
X_3	6	15	8	8	6	9	17	22	18	4	23	9	8

Calculate the product moment correlation coefficient between X_1 and X_3;

(d) Test, at the 1% significance level, the hypothesis that there is no linear association between X_1 and X_3;

(e) Write down two noticeable features of the correlation matrix. [A]

Key point summary

1 A hypothesis test needs two hypotheses identified at the beginning: **H₀** the **null hypothesis** and **H₁** the **alternative hypothesis**.   *p26*

H₀ and **H₁** both refer to the population from which the sample is taken.

H₀ states what is to be assumed true unless overwhelming evidence proves otherwise. In the case of testing the PMCC, **H₀** is $\rho = 0$.

2 **H₀** states that a situation is unchanged, that a population parameter takes its usual value.   *p26*

H₁ states that the parameter has increased, decreased or just changed.

3 A **two-tailed** test involves testing for any (non-directional) change in a parameter.   *p27*
A **one-tailed** test involves testing for a specific increase or decrease (change in one direction only).

A **two-tailed test** results in a critical region with two areas. A **one-tailed test** results in a critical region in one area.

4 The **critical region** or **critical value** identifies the range of extreme values which lead to the **rejection** of **H₀**.   *p29*

If the **test statistic** lies **in** the **critical region** or beyond the **critical value H₀** is rejected.

5 The **significance level** of a test is the probability that a test statistic lies in the extreme critical region, on the assumption **H₀** is true. It determines the level of overwhelming evidence deemed necessary for the rejection of **H₀**.   *p34*

The **significance level** is commonly, but not exclusively, set at 5%.

6 The general procedure for hypothesis testing is: p34
  1 Write down H_0 and H_1.
  2 Decide which test to use.
  3 Decide on the significance level.
  4 Identify the critical region.
  5 Calculate the test statistic.
  6 Make your conclusion.

  The **critical value** is often found directly from statistical tables as in the case of testing a PMCC.

7 Errors which can occur are: p36
  A **Type 1** error which is to reject H_0 when it actually is true.
  A **Type 2** error which is to accept H_0 when it actually is not true.

Test yourself	What to review
1 Which of the following alternative hypotheses would require a one-tailed test and which a two-tailed test ?	*Section 2.2*
(a) Amphetamines stimulate motor performance and median reaction times decrease for those subjects who have taken amphetamine tablets;	
(b) There is a correlation between the age of a toad and the number of speckles found on it;	
(c) Patients suffering from asthma have a higher median health conscious index than people who do not suffer from asthma.	
2 What is the name given to the value with which a test statistic is compared in order to decide whether a null hypothesis should be rejected ?	*Section 2.3*
3 (a) What is the name given to the level of extreme probability at which it is agreed that the null hypothesis will be rejected?	*Section 2.3*
(b) What is the value of the most common conventional level used for this extreme probability?	
4 A manufacturer collects data on the age and the annual maintenance costs for his 12 welding machines. The product moment correlation coefficient between age and cost is found to be 0.874. Stating clearly your null and alternative hypotheses and using a 5% significance level, test whether there is any evidence of a direct association between age and maintenance costs for these machines.	*Sections 2.1 and 2.3*

Test yourself (*continued*)	**What to review**

5 At the end of their first year on a college course, students take several exams, two of which are sociology and research methods. The product moment correlation coefficient is evaluated between the sociology and the research methods scores for a randomly chosen selection of 15 students. This coefficient was evaluated as -0.675.

Sections 2.1 and 2.3

    (a) State clearly the null and alternative hypotheses to be used in testing for an inverse association between the scores of students in sociology and in research methods;

    (b) Carry out this test using a 1% significance level and state clearly your conclusion.

6 The product moment correlation coefficient between the brain mass and liver mass for a random sample of 15 mice is found. This value is to be tested using a 5% significance level to determine whether there is an association between the masses in mice.

Section 2.5

    (a) Within what range of values would it be necessary for r, the sample correlation coefficient, to lie in order to conclude that an association does indeed exist between brain and liver mass?

    (b) What is the meaning of:
        (i) a Type 1 error,   **(ii)** a Type 2 error,
in the context of this question ?

Test yourself ANSWERS

1 (a) 1 tail;   **(b)** 2 tail;   **(c)** 1 tail.

2 Critical value.

3 (a) significance level;   **(b)** 5%.

4 $H_0 \ p = 0$, $\alpha = 0.05$,   1 tail.
  $H_1 \ p > 0$, $n = 12$,   ts $= 0.874$,   cv $= 0.497$.
  Reject H_0: significant evidence of direct association between age and maintenance costs.

5 (a) $H_0 \ p = 0$, $H_1 \ p < 0$;
  (b) ts $= -0.675$, $\alpha = 0.01$,   cv $= -0.592$ 1 tail $n = 15$.
  Reject H_0: significant evidence of inverse association between sociology and research scores.

6 $n = 15$
  (a) $\alpha = 0.02$,   2 tail,   cv $= -0.514$,
  range $-1 \leqslant r \leqslant -0.514$, $0.514 \leqslant r \leqslant 1$.
  (b) (i) Type 1 error → conclude an association does exist between brain mass and liver mass when, in fact, it does not exist,
    (ii) Type 2 error → conclude no association exists between brain mass and liver mass when, in fact, a significant association does exist.

CHAPTER 3

Rank correlation

Learning objectives

In Chapter 8 of S1, the concept of correlation was introduced. This chapter extends this concept to include rank correlation and the procedures involved in hypothesis testing of a rank correlation coefficient.

After studying this chapter you should be able to:

- evaluate a Spearman's rank correlation coefficient
- understand the link between Spearman's rank and the product moment correlation coefficients
- test the hypothesis that a rank correlation coefficient is equal to zero.

3.1 Spearman's rank correlation coefficient, r_s

Consider the following example which will introduce rank correlation.

Worked example 3.1

At a film festival in the South of France, two experienced judges are each asked to view seven films in the 'Comedy' category and put them in rank order where a rank of 1 is given to the best of the seven films and a rank of 7 is given to the one judged to be the worst.

The following results were obtained:

Film	1	2	3	4	5	6	7
Judge A(x)	7	3	1	4	2	5	6
Judge B(y)	1	2	6	7	4	3	5

Find the value of the correlation coefficient between the rankings of the two judges and comment on your result.

Solution

The data given here differ from that in Chapter 8 of S1 where the bivariate data given were measured variables or scores **not** *ranks* as is the case in this example.

However, the value of the correlation coefficient between the ranks of the two judges can be found in the same way as before using the formula

$$r = \frac{S_{XY}}{\sqrt{S_{XX} \times S_{YY}}}$$

$$S_{XY} = \frac{100}{7} - (4 \times 4) = \frac{-12}{7}$$

$$S_{XX} = \frac{140}{7} - (4^2) = 4$$

and

$$S_{YY} = \frac{140}{7} - (4^2) = 4$$

So $\quad r = \dfrac{\dfrac{-12}{7}}{\sqrt{4 \times 4}} = \dfrac{-3}{7} = -0.42857 = -0.429 \text{ (3 sf)}$

As before, the value of r can be found directly from a calculator and this is the easiest way to evaluate it.

Note that S_{XX} and S_{YY} are the same, both equal to 4, because the x and y values are the same seven rank values 1 to 7.

The correlation coefficient between the ranks is called **Spearman's rank correlation coefficient** and is usually denoted r_s. In this case it indicates that the two judges do not seem to agree in their opinions of the films since it is **negative.** It would appear that Judge A thinks highly of some films which Judge B does not like very much at all.

Just as with the product moment correlation coefficient, this measure of correlation always lies in the range:

$$-1 \leqslant r_s \leqslant +1$$

> Spearman's rank correlation coefficient, r_s, provides a measure of the association between the **rank orders** of two variables.

3.2 Alternative formula for r_s

In the formulae book on page 15, a quite different formula is given for the Spearman's rank correlation coefficient, r_s. This formula is equivalent to the calculation above, but uses the sums of simple series, since rank values are involved, to simplify the formula to

$$r_s = 1 - \frac{6\sum d^2}{n(n^2 - 1)}$$

where d represents the difference between the rank values and n is the sample size.

Film	1	2	3	4	5	6	7
Judge A(x)	7	3	1	4	2	5	6
Judge B(y)	1	2	6	7	4	3	5
d*	6	1	5	3	2	2	1

*Since the values for d are all squared, just the positive values for d, or $|d|$, are given in the table opposite.

$\sum d^2 = 6^2 + 1^2 + 5^2 + 3^2 + 2^2 + 1^2 = 80$ and $n = 7$

So $r_s = 1 - \dfrac{6 \times 80}{7 \times 48} = \dfrac{-3}{7} = -0.429 \text{ (3 sf)}$ as before.

In practice, finding r_s directly from a calculator, using the rank values, is easier than using this formula and is the recommended method.

> Spearman's rank correlation coefficient can be obtained from the **rank values** of data, either by using the formula
>
> $$r_s = 1 - \frac{6\sum d^2}{n(n^2 - 1)}$$
>
> or by obtaining the value of the product moment correlation coefficient between these rank values directly from the calculator.
>
> If the data contains ties the two methods give slightly different results. The PMCC between rank values is correct but either values will be accepted in an examination.

Worked example 3.2

Eight contestants enter a writing competition for short stories. Two judges place these contestants in the following order where a rank value of 1 is given to the best story and a rank value of 8 to the one least liked by the judge.

The results are in the table below:

Contestant	A	B	C	D	E	F	G	H
Judge 1(x)	8	6	7	2	4	3	5	1
Judge 2(y)	5	2	4	8	1	6	7	3

Calculate the coefficient of rank correlation and comment on your result.

Solution

Using the formula for Spearman's rank correlation coefficient:

$$r_s = 1 - \frac{6\sum d^2}{n(n^2 - 1)}$$

Contestant	A	B	C	D	E	F	G	H
Judge 1(x)	8	6	7	2	4	3	5	1
Judge 2(y)	5	2	4	8	1	6	7	3
d		3	4	3	6	3	3	2	2

> Alternatively the rank values can be entered into your calculator and r_s obtained directly. You are recommended to do this in the exam.

$n = 8 \qquad \sum d^2 = 3^2 + 4^2 + 3^2 + 6^2 + 3^2 + 3^2 + 2^2 + 2^2 = 96$

So $r_s = 1 - \dfrac{6 \times 96}{8 \times 63} = -\dfrac{1}{7} = -0.143$

This value for the rank correlation coefficient is very close to zero and indicates little connection between the rank values assigned to each story by the two judges. They appear to have very different opinions about which stories are the best.

Worked example 3.3

Data is gathered on the number of television licences per 1000 of population and the level of cinema admissions per head per year in ten large towns in the North of the UK. The figures are given in the following table:

Town	A	B	C	D	E	F	G	H	J	K
TV licences per 1000	220	80	160	290	395	75	300	325	440	340
Number of cinema admissions per head	10.8	12.1	12.5	12.2	8.8	13.5	10.0	9.5	9.2	10.5

3

(a) Explain the differences and the similarities between the product moment correlation coefficient and Spearman's rank correlation coefficient;

(b) Calculate the value of Spearman's rank correlation coefficient for the above data.

Solution

(a) For the product moment correlation coefficent, the paired data must be scores or measured items. For Spearman's rank coefficient, the data involved must be rank order values. The product moment correlation coefficient measures how close the given bivariate data is to a straight line relationship. Spearman's rank coefficient quantifies how closely connected the bivariate data is with respect to rank order. Both coefficients can range from -1 to $+1$.

(b) The data given is not rank order values and therefore the given data has to be replaced with its rank order values to enable Spearman's rank correlation coefficient to be calculated. In the table below, the rank values are substituted for the original given measured values.

Town	A	B	C	D	E	F	G	H	J	K
Rank TV licences	7	9	8	6	2	10	5	4	1	3
Rank no. of cinema admissions	5	4	2	3	10	1	7	8	9	6
d	2	5	6	3	8	9	2	4	8	3

$n = 8$ $\sum d^2 = 4 + 25 + 36 + 9 + 64 + 81 + 4 + 16 + 64 + 9 = 312$

So $r_s = 1 - \dfrac{6 \times 312}{10 \times 99} = -\dfrac{49}{55} = -0.891$

> Again, by entering the rank values into your calculator you can obtain the value for r_s directly.

The value of r_s is fairly close to -1 and therefore this rank coefficient indicates a close inverse connection in the rank order values for TV licences and cinema admissions. It would seem that towns where there are high numbers of TV licences per head tend to be those where there are lower cinema admissions.

Worked example 3.4

A wine taster is given nine bottles of wine to try in a blind tasting experiment. She is asked to place these wines in order of preference (rank 1 for the best) and these results are shown below, together with the price of each bottle.

Bottle	A	B	C	D	E	F	G	H	J
Price (p)	295	345	395	445	595	595	650	775	950
Rank	8	7	4	9	1	6	2	3	5

Calculate the value of Spearman's rank correlation coefficient between the rank order value for the wine and its price. Comment on the value of this correlation coefficient.

Solution

The preferences of the taster are already ranked but the prices of the bottles are given as their actual values, not rank values, and therefore these need to be put in rank order.

Note that two bottles of wine are the same price and the usual convention for tied ranks is followed.

Bottle	A	B	C	D	E	F	G	H	J
Price (p)	9	8	7	6	4.5	4.5	3	2	1
Rank	8	7	4	9	1	6	2	3	5
d	1	1	3	3	3.5	1.5	1	1	4

> The convention for tied ranks is that the *average* rank value, for those which tie, should be assigned to each reading. In this case, ranks 4 and 5 tie so each value is assigned the rank 4.5.

$$n = 9 \quad \sum d^2 = 1 + 1 + 9 + 9 + 12.25 + 2.25 + 1 + 1 + 16 = 52.5$$

$$\text{So } r_s = 1 - \frac{6 \times 52.5}{9 \times 80} = \frac{9}{16} = 0.5625$$

This value for r_s indicates a fair, direct connection between the rank order values for preference and for price. It appears that those wines preferred most by the taster often tended to be the more expensive ones. However, this rule was not always the case and some of the cheaper wines were quite highly rated.

> If you directly put these rank values into the calculator, the value for r_s is slightly different because of the tied ranks. The calculator value is $r_s = 0.561$. This is the correct value, but **either** value is acceptable in the exam.

EXERCISE 3A

1 A child was asked to rank seven types of sweet according to preference and to sweetness with the following results:

Type	1	2	3	4	5	6	7
Preference	3	4	1	2	6	5	7
Sweetness	2	3	4	1	5	6	7

Calculate Spearman's rank correlation coefficient for these data. Comment on your result.

2 A food critic tastes eight supermarket instant ready meals and puts the meals in rank order of preference where rank 1 indicates the meal he considered to be the best.
The results, together with the prices of the meals are given in the table below:

Brand	A	B	C	D	E	F	G	H
Rank preference	5	4	6	7	8	1	2	3
Price (p)	171	165	127	150	143	139	149	179

Calculate the value of Spearman's rank correlation coefficient between the rank and of preference and the price of the meals.

3 Nine chrysanthemums were ranked by a judge according to their colour and their overall appearance. The results are shown below:

Flower	1	2	3	4	5	6	7	8	9
Colour	2	1	9	4	8	7	6	5	3
Overall	6	5	7	2	4	9	1	3	8

Find the value of the rank correlation coefficient between the colour and the overall appearance of the flowers.

4 The table below gives the number of rotten peaches in 10 randomly selected crates from a large consignment after they had been kept in storage for a stated number of days.

Days in storage	6	6	14	21	24	29	30	35	38	40
Number of rotten peaches	3	8	8	6	15	11	13	17	18	21

Calculate Spearman's rank correlation coefficient for these data and comment on your findings.

5 A group of students attempt an assignment consisting of two questions. The scores on each question for a random sample of eight of this group are given below.

Student	1	2	3	4	5	6	7	8
Question 1	42	68	32	84	71	55	55	70
Question 2	39	75	43	79	83	65	62	68

(a) Calculate the Spearman's rank correlation coefficient between the scores on the two questions;

(b) Give an interpretation of your result.

6 A group of students were assessed by written examination, practical work and essay. The following table shows the examination %, practical work grade and the essay rank (best essay ranked 1) as judged by the course tutor.

Student	G	H	I	J	K	L	M	N
Exam %	62	43	57	84	41	17	29	66
Practical grade	A−	C	C+	A	C−	B+	D	B+
Essay rank	2	6	4	1	7	5	8	3

(a) Calculate Spearman's rank correlation coefficient between:
    (i) exam % and practical grade,
    (ii) exam and essay rank,
    (iii) practical grade and essay rank;

(b) Comment on the performance of student L;

(c) It is suggested that next year only examination mark and practical work grade should be recorded. Comment;

(d) Why is Spearman's rank more suitable than the product moment correlation coefficient for these data? [A]

3.3 Testing a hypothesis about Spearman's rank correlation coefficient

In Section 2.3 of Chapter 2, the procedure for testing whether a population product moment correlation coefficient is significantly different from zero was introduced. In exactly the same way, a test can be carried out to determine whether a population Spearman's Rank correlation coefficient is significantly different from zero.

The critical values for testing a Spearman's rank correlation coefficient are found in Table 9 of the formulae book. On comparison, it can be seen that the values given are slightly lower than those in Table 8 which relate to values of the product moment correlation coefficient, although for large samples there is hardly any difference.

In the same way as a product moment correlation coefficient is tested, the sample rank correlation coefficient is compared with the critical value obtained from Table 9 for the appropriate significance level and the sample size n.

A test can be carried out to determine whether an association between rank orders of two variables exists in the population. The null hypothesis:

$$\mathbf{H_0}\ \rho_s = 0$$

The critical value is found from Table 9.

The critical values for testing Spearman's rank correlation coefficient are different than for the PMCC. This is because the PMCC values assume that the data follows a bivariate normal distribution. This will not be true if the data consists of ranks.

Because r_s is calculated from ranks it can only take certain values (it is a discrete variable) and so it is not usually possible to obtain critical values with exactly the required significance level. The critical values given, in Table 9, are those with significance levels **closest** to the value stated. This means that the value tabulated for 5% may give a significance level which is not exactly 5% but is a little less or a little more.

In Table 8, the critical values relate to the exact significance level since r is a **continuous** variable.

In practice, the critical values found in Table 9 will be used in exactly the same way as they were when found using Table 8.

Worked example 3.5

In a major art competition, two judges award scores out of a total of 40 to the eight finalists. The scores given to these eight finalists are:

Painting	1	2	3	4	5	6	7	8
Judge A	39	23	25	35	37	36	26	30
Judge B	36	16	28	30	31	24	19	20

Calculate the value of Spearman's rank correlation coefficient between the scores given by the two judges.
Stating clearly the null and alternative hypotheses used, test whether there is any evidence of an association between the two judgements.

Solution

The rank values for the above data are given below:

Painting	1	2	3	4	5	6	7	8
Judge A	1	8	7	4	2	3	6	5
Judge B	1	8	4	3	2	5	7	6

Directly from entering these ranks into the calculator, it can be found that $r_s = 0.810$.

$H_0 \; \rho_s = 0$ pop Spearman's rank correlation is zero.
$H_0 \; \rho_s \neq 0$ pop Spearman's rank correlation not zero.

From Table 9, the critical value for a sample where $n = 8$, two-tailed at 5% is 0.7381.
The test statistic is $r_s = 0.810$.

In this case, $|r_s| > 0.7381$ and so there is significant evidence to reject H_0 and conclude that there is an association in the rank order of the scores between the two judges. The paintings to which Judge A awarded higher scores were also those awarded higher scores by Judge B. The two judges seem to agree fairly well in their opinions of the paintings.

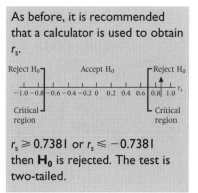

As before, it is recommended that a calculator is used to obtain r_s.

$r_s \geq 0.7381$ or $r_s \leq -0.7381$ then H_0 is rejected. The test is two-tailed.

Worked example 3.6

Two children were asked to score 10 chocolate bars according to their sweetness. The scores were on a scale of 1 to 10 where 1 is the least sweet and 10 the sweetest. One of the children scored the bars in the reverse order by mistake.

The results are shown:

(a) Calculate the Spearman's rank correlation coefficient between the scores of the two children;

(b) Stating clearly your null and alternative hypotheses, test, at the 5% level, whether there is an inverse association between the rank values of the sweetness scores given the two children.

Bar	Child 1	Child 2
A	3	5
B	4	10
C	1	9
D	6	6
E	2	8
F	7	1
G	5	7
H	7	4
I	9	3
K	8	2

Solution

The original data is not given as rank values and so the data must be put in rank order. The ranks are given in the table below. A rank value of 1 is assigned to the highest score (the sweetest) and a rank value of 10 to the least sweet.

Bar	Child 1	Child 2	d
A	8	6	2
B	7	1	6
C	10	2	8
D	5	5	0
E	9	3	6
F	3.5	10	6.5
G	6	4	2
H	3.5	7	3.5
I	1	8	7
J	2	9	7

Directly from the calculator, the value for r_s can be obtained. In this case, $r_s = -0.802$.

Using the formula, $\sum d^2 = 296.5$ and so,

$$r_s = 1 - \frac{(6 \times 296.5)}{(10 \times 99)} = -0.797$$

$$\mathbf{H_o}\ \rho_s = 0$$

$$\mathbf{H_1}\ \rho_s < 0$$

The critical value from Table 9 for a one-tailed test using a 5% significance level for a sample where $n = 10$ is -0.5636.
In this case $r_s = -0.802$ (or -0.797) and $r_s < -0.5636$.

We conclude that $\mathbf{H_0}$ is rejected and there is evidence of an inverse association between the rank order values of sweetness given to the chocolate bars by the two children.
The bars which child A scored higher for sweetness, child B tended to score lower.

Note here that there are tied ranks. Child 1 gave bars F and H the same score of 7. The rank values 3 and 4 are therefore averaged and a rank of 3.5 given to each.

In the case of tied ranks, the formula gives a slightly different result to that obtained directly from the calculator. This does not affect the conclusion of the hypothesis test. Both methods are given in the example and both are equally acceptable in the exam. However the value obtained directly from the calculator is the correct one.

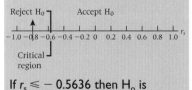

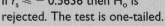

If $r_s \leqslant -0.5636$ then H_o is rejected. The test is one-tailed.

EXERCISE 3B

1 Stating clearly the null and alternative hypotheses you are using, test the following Spearman's rank correlation coefficients to determine whether there is:

(a) an association between preference for and price of ready meals as given in Question **2** of Exercise 3A. Use a 5% significance level;

(b) a direct association between preference and sweetness using the data given in Question **1** of Exercise 3A. Use a 1% significance level;

(c) a direct association between colour and overall appearance rating using the data given in Question **3** of Exercise 3A. Use a 1% significance level;

(d) an association between number of days in storage and number of rotten peaches using the data of Question **4** of Exercise 3A. Use a 1% significance level.

2 The five finalists in a piano competition were placed in the following order by the two judges:

	1st	2nd	3rd	4th	5th
Judge 1	C	E	D	A	B
Judge 2	B	C	A	D	E

Evaluate the Spearman's rank correlation coefficient for these data.

Stating the null and alternative hypothesis used, test, at the 5% significance level, for an inverse association between the opinions of the judges and comment.

3 The following table shows the percenage of part-time staff employed by nine supermarkets in a large city and their rankings in terms of weekly takings.

Part-time staff, %	45	56	38	29	54	33	36	33	22
Weekly takings, rank	7	4	5	9	2	8	1	3	6

Calculate the value of Spearman's rank correlation coefficient for this set of data. Test, at the 5% significance level, the hypothesis that there is no relationship between the percentage of part-time staff employed and weekly takings.

4 The reading age of a random sample of eight children entering secondary school was recorded. During their first weeks their English teacher asked them to write a poem. The reading ages and the ranks of the poems, as judged by the English teacher are shown in the following table.

Reading age	8.7	11.2	14.4	6.8	12.3	13.1	9.6	10.8
Rank of poem	7	4	3	8	1	6	5	2

Calculate Spearman's rank correlation coefficient and test, at the 1% significance level, for an association between reading age and ability to write poetry.

5 Rainfall, x cm, and hours of sunshine, y, on nine randomly selected October days is shown in the table below.

x	1.3	3.8	4.2	2.6	2.1	2.6	5.3	0.0	0.9
y	1.5	0.3	0.0	4.2	3.6	0.5	0.0	6.2	1.4

Calculate Spearman's rank correlation coefficient. Investigate, at the 5% significance level, whether days with high rainfall tend to have few hours of sunshine.

3.4 Relationship between product moment and Spearman's rank correlation coefficients

In some cases, the values of r and r_s are very similar and both will lead to the conclusion that there is an association between the two variables in the population. In this case, a scatter diagram will show a clear linear relationship.

> As you saw in S1, Chapter 8.4, it is always useful to refer to a scatter diagram when interpreting correlation coefficients.

However, sometimes the value of $|r_s|$ is much greater than the value of $|r|$. This is a clear indication that there is a non-linear relationship between the two variables which can be seen by referring to a scatter diagram.

Consider the following data which gives test results for nine students selected at random from Year 8 at a large high school. The table also shows the rank values in brackets.

Student	Maths	English	Physics
1	9 (9)	59 (1)	4 (9)
2	41 (6)	38 (4)	17 (6)
3	49 (5)	39 (3)	32 (5)
4	18 (8)	51 (2)	11 (8)
5	52 (4)	31 (6)	43 (4)
6	63 (1)	23 (9)	74 (2)
7	62 (2)	30 (7)	83 (1)
8	32 (7)	36 (5)	14 (7)
9	58 (3)	24 (8)	55 (3)

> Values of the correlation coefficients are obtained directly from a calculator.

The scatter diagram illustrates the students' results in maths and English.

The value of the product moment correlation coefficient is $r = -0.941$.

The value of the Spearman's rank correlation coefficient is $r_s = -0.917$.

Both coefficients are fairly similar and indicate a strong inverse relationship between the results in maths and English for Year 8 students.

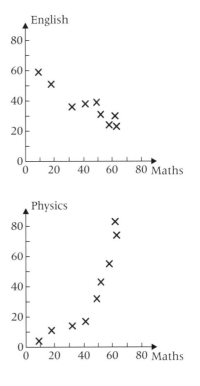

The second scatter diagram is for results in maths and in physics.

The value of the product moment correlation coefficient is $r = 0.894$.

The value of the Spearman's rank correlation coefficient is $r_s = 0.983$.

$| r_s |$ is much larger than $| r |$ and the scatter diagram reveals the non-linear relationship.

MIXED EXERCISE

1 A clothing manufacturer collected the following data on the maintenance costs and age of his sewing machines.

Sewing machine	Maintenance cost (£)	Age (months)
1	24	13
2	144	75
3	110	64
4	63	52
5	240	90
6	20	15
7	40	35
8	180	82
9	42	25
10	50	46
11	92	50

(a) Plot a scatter diagram of the data;

(b) Calculate the product moment correlation coefficient;

(c) Calculate the Spearman's rank correlation coefficient;

(d) Stating clearly the null and alternative hypotheses used, carry out two tests, using your results from **(b)** and **(c)**, to determine whether there appears to be an association between age and costs of sewing machines.
Use a 1% significance level for each test.

2 The following data show the IQ and the score in an English test of a random sample of 10 pupils taken from a mixed ability Year group.

Pupil	IQ	English (%)
A	110	52
B	107	62
C	127	74
D	100	40
E	132	70
F	130	68
G	98	46
H	109	76
I	114	62
J	124	72

(a) Find the product moment correlation coefficient;

(b) Stating clearly the null and alternative hypotheses used, test whether there is a direct association between IQ and English score. Use a 5% significance level;

For another group of eight randomly selected pupils from the mixed ability Year group, their teacher assessed each pupil according to their aptitude for schoolwork and their perseverance. A rating scale of 0 to 100 was used.

Pupil	Aptitude	Perseverance
K	42	73
L	68	39
M	32	63
N	84	49
O	71	83
P	55	65
Q	58	62
R	70	68

(c) Find the Spearman's rank correlation coefficient for these data;

(d) Stating clearly the null and alternative hypotheses used, test whether there is an association between aptitude and perseverance. Use a 5% significance level;

(e) Comment on your findings in **(b)** and **(c)**.   [A]

3 A company employing sales representatives wishes to assess the correlation between their scores obtained during training and during their first few years of service.
During training, points are awarded – these reflect efficiency at work, punctuality, appearance, etc. Once working for the company, points are awarded for the amount of business brought in, number of contacts made, customer responses, etc. Total scores are found from these points.

For a random sample of 12 sales representatives, the training and service scores awarded by one manager in the company are given in the following table.

Sales representative	Training score	Service score
A	10	11
B	15	11
C	20	27
D	19	25
E	9	11
F	12	13
G	11	14
H	7	9
I	18	15
J	21	26
K	12	20
L	17	18

(a) Calculate the Spearman's rank correlation coefficient for the data;

(b) Stating clearly the null and alternative hypotheses used, test for a direct association between training and service scores awarded by this manager. Use a 5% significance level.
Interpret your findings in the context of this question;

(c) A second manager also assessed the same 12 sales representatives. This manager agreed with the service scores awarded but awarded very different training scores. The Spearman's rank correlation coefficient resulting from the scores awarded by the second manager was -0.808.
Carry out a test using a 5% significance level to determine whether there appears to be an association between the scores awarded by the second manager. Comment on your findings. [A]

4 The following data show the annual income per head, x ($\$$) and the infant mortality, y (per 1000 live births) for a sample of 11 countries.

Country	x	y
A	130	150
B	5950	43
C	560	121
D	2010	53
E	1870	41
F	170	169
G	390	143
H	580	59
I	820	75
J	6620	20
K	3800	39

(a) Draw a scatter diagram for the data and describe the relationship between income and infant mortality as suggested by the scatter diagram;

(b) An economist asks you to calculate the product moment correlation coefficient.
   (i) Carry out this calculation,
   (ii) Explain briefly to the economist why this calculation may not be appropriate;

(c) Calculate Spearman's rank correlation coefficient for this data;

(d) Stating clearly the null and alternative hypotheses used, test to see whether there is an association in rank orders between income and infant mortality. Use a 1% significance level;

(e) Comment and compare the values of the two correlation coefficients you have calculated.   [A]

*5 A consumer company tests 10 microwave ovens and awards a grade according to their efficiency when used for various tasks. The grade awarded for efficiency is given in the following table, together with the price and the rank order value given for the overall appearance of each oven.

Oven	Efficiency grade	Price (£)	Appearance rank
1	A	256	3
2	C	149	6
3	D	150	9
4	B$^+$	199	4
5	C	175	7
6	E	142	10
7	D	177	8
8	B$^+$	185	1
9	B	190	5
10	A$^+$	275	2

(a) Calculate Spearman's rank correlation coefficient between:
   (i) price and efficiency grade,
   (ii) price and appearance ranking;

(b) Investigate, at the 1% significance level, whether the price and the efficiency grades are related.
   State clearly the null and alternative hypotheses used;

(c) It is suggested that a wider range of models of oven should be investigated but that appearance ranking should not be used. Comment on this suggestion with reference to your results in (a) and (b);

(d) Comment also on the suggestion that the product moment correlation coefficient between price and efficiency grade should be calculated.   [A]

*6 The length of service and the gross earnings of a sample of 11 employees of a large store in 1984, are given below:

Employee	A	B	C	D	E	F	G	H	J	K	L
Length of service (months)	132	64	28	117	94	14	17	19	76	21	18
Gross earnings 1984 (£)	8220	6140	4890	7410	5930	4720	13 680	4320	6490	5070	4760

(a) Plot a scatter diagram of these data;

(b) Calculate the product moment correlation coefficient;

(c) Calculate Spearman's rank correlation coefficient;

(d) Use your result in part **(c)** to test, at the 5% significance level, whether gross annual earnings are associated with length of service;

(e) Describe the relationship (if any) between length of service and gross earnings suggested by the scatter diagram and comment on the values of the two correlation coefficients calculated. [A]

*7 An instrument panel is being designed to control a complex industrial process. It will be necessary to use both hands independently to operate the panel. To help with the design it was decided to time a number of operators, each carrying out the same task once with the left hand and once with the right hand.

The times, in seconds, were as follows:

Operator	A	B	C	D	E	F	G	H	I	J	K
l.h., x	49	58	63	42	27	55	39	33	72	66	50
r.h., y	34	37	49	27	49	40	66	21	64	42	37

(a) Plot a scatter diagram of the data;

(b) Calculate the product moment correlation coefficient between the two variables and comment on this value;

(c) Test, at the 5% significance level, for an association between times with left hand and times with right hand;

(d) Further investigation revealed that two of the operators were left handed. State, giving a reason, which you think these were. Omitting their two results, calculate Spearman's rank correlation coefficient and test for an association;

(e) What can you say about the relationship between the times to carry out the task with left and right hands? [A]

*8 The following table is derived from the 1991 Census. It gives the values of three variables X, Y and Z in eight different areas of the United Kingdom.

X is the percentage of households living in owner-occupied accommodation.
Y is the number in thousands of adults with higher educational qualifications.
Z is the population in thousands.

Area	X	Y	Z
1	51	11.9	150
2	32	37.0	746
3	49	43.7	662
4	33	10.6	345
5	73	36.4	239
6	57	8.2	108
7	52	15.3	210
8	77	28.6	223

(a) Calculate the product moment correlation between X and Y and comment on its value;

(b) Assuming the data may be regarded as a random sample from a bivariate normal distribution with correlation coefficient ρ, test, at the 5% significance level, whether ρ differs from zero;

(c) Calculate Spearman's rank correlation coefficient between Y and Z;

(d) Test, using a 5% significance level, whether the number of adults with higher educational qualifications in an area is associated with the population of the area;

(e) Form a new variable, W, expressing Y as a percentage of Z. Plot a scatter diagram of the variables X and W;

(f) The product moment correlation coefficient between X and W is 0.941. Compare this value with that between X and Y and discuss your results. [A]

*9 A group of students planned to share a house whilst at university. They identified 12 possible houses and used a map to measure the straight line distance, x km, of each house from the Student Union. They then measured the road distance, y km, of each house from the Student Union. The distances are shown below.

House	A	B	C	D	E	F	G	H	I	J	K	L
Straight line distance, x	7.5	3.0	23.5	13.4	9.3	9.1	9.8	3.7	17.9	4.7	2.0	2.4
Road distance, y	8.8	3.2	28.4	16.7	9.5	8.9	12.4	9.9	22.5	4.9	2.5	2.9

(a) Draw a scatter diagram of the data;

(b) A statistician recommended that houses F and H should be omitted from any further analysis as she suspected errors in their data. Discuss why she made this recommendation and, for each house, the strength of the evidence supporting her suspicions;

(c) The houses, in the table on the previous page, have been presented in order of preference. That is, the students would prefer to live in house A, followed by B, etc. Omitting houses F and H calculate the value of Spearman's rank correlation coefficient between preference and road distance from the Student Union. Investigate, using a 5% significance level, whether the ranks are related.   [A]

*10 As part of an investigation into fashion, a number of passers-by were shown six garments and asked to estimate the price being asked for identical garments at a nearby boutique.

Garment	P	Q	R	S	T	U
Price estimated by Sonia, £z	35	28	55	25	50	60
Price estimated by Jason, £y	14	22	40	75	30	80

(a) Calculate the product moment correlation coefficient between the estimates made by Jason and the estimates made by Sonia. Assuming the data comes from a bivariate normal distribution with correlation coefficient ρ, test the hypothesis that $\rho = 0$. Use a 5% significance level.

The estimates of five other passers-by, A, B, C, D and E, were also recorded. Analysis then revealed the following.
The product moment correlation coefficient between the estimates of A and B was -0.3.
The product moment correlation coefficient between the estimates of B and C was 1.
Spearman's rank correlation coefficient between the estimates of C and D was -1.
Spearman's rank correlation coefficient between the estimates of D and E was 0.7;

(b) In **each** of the following, either state the value of the correlation coefficient or state that there is insufficient information to evaluate it.
   (i) Product moment correlation coefficient between the estimates of A and C,
   (ii) Product moment correlation coefficient between the estimates of A and D,
   (iii) Spearman's rank correlation coefficient between the estimates of A and D,
   (iv) Spearman's rank correlation coefficient between the estimates of B and E.   [A]

*11 In a study of electronic calculators, an index was devised to measure the variety and complexity of the operations they were capable of performing. The value of the index for 10 different calculators together with their selling price is given below.

(a) Plot a scatter diagram of the data;

(b) Calculate Spearman's rank correlation coefficient;

(c) Give a reason why it is more appropriate to calculate Spearman's rank rather than the product moment correlation coefficient for this set of data;

Selling price, £x	10	40	60	92	109	120	128	160	164	170
Index, y		15	38	27	70	98	170	162	305	485	599

(d) Stating clearly your null and alternative hypotheses, investigate each of the following claims:
   (i) selling price is associated with the value of the index. Use a 10% significance level,
   (ii) high selling price is associated with high values of the index. Use a 1% significance level,
   (iii) high selling price is associated with low values of the index. Use a 5% significance level;

(e) Explain why it was unnecessary to identify the critical value in part **(d)(iii)**. [A]

Key point summary

1 Spearman's rank correlation coefficient, r_s, provides a measure of the association between the rank orders of two variables. If the data is not given as rank order values, then it must be put into rank order before calculations are carried out.   *p45*

2 Spearman's rank correlation coefficient can be obtained from the **rank values** of data, either by using the formula   *p46*

$$r_s = 1 - \frac{6\sum d^2}{n(n^2 - 1)}$$

where d is the difference in rank order values for each pair and n is the number of pairs in the sample; or by obtaining the value of the product moment correlation coefficient between these rank values directly from the calculator. This is the **recommended** method.

If the data contains ties the two methods give slightly different results. The PMCC between rank values is correct but either value will be accepted in an examination.

3 A test can be carried out to determine whether an association between rank orders of two variables exists in the population. The null hypothesis is:

p50

$$\mathbf{H_0} \; \rho_s = 0$$

The critical value is found from Table 9.

Test yourself	**What to review**

1 In each of the two cases given below, a correlation coefficient is going to be evaluated in order to determine whether there is an association between the two variables involved. State, for each example, whether the Spearman's rank or the product moment coefficient would be the appropriate measure to evaluate.

Section 3.1

(a) Ranking of two ski jumps for style in a competition with six competitors.

Person	1	2	3	4	5	6
Jump A	4	1	6	2	3	5
Jump B	3	2	6	5	1	4

(b) Length of two ski jumps in a competition with six competitors.

Person	1	2	3	4	5	6
Length A	84	91	86	94	82	79
Length B	91	88	78	91	87	85

2 A tea taster is given seven infusions of tea leaves to put in order of preference. The price per kilo of the leaves is also put in rank order with the following results:

Sections 3.1 and 3.2

Tea	**Preference**	**Price**
A	4	3
B	2.5	1
C	1	2
D	6	6
E	2.5	4
F	7	5
G	5	7

(a) Why do the ranks 2.5 appear in the preference column for teas B and E?

(b) Calculate the value of the Spearman's rank correlation coefficient between preference and price;

(c) Comment on your result.

Test yourself (*continued*)	What to review
3 Suggest a reason why a value for the Spearman's rank correlation coefficient for a set of paired data may be much higher than the value of the product moment coefficient for the same data.	*Section 3.4*

4 Assign rank order values to the following data where it is appropriate to do so. If the data is already suitably ranked, it should be left in this form.

(a)

Pupil	1	2	3	4	5	6
Drama grade	A	A+	C	D	B	E
Exam score	73	82	46	55	61	44

Section 3.1

(b)

Cake	1	2	3	4	5	6
Price	49	85	65	75	45	50
Preference rank	3	2	6	5	1	4

5 Find the Spearman's rank correlation coefficient between: *Section 3.3*
  (a) the drama grade and exam score in question **4(a)**;
  (b) the price and the preference rank in question **4(b)**;
  (c) stating the null and alternative hypotheses used, carry out a test to determine whether, at a 5% significance level, there is evidence of association between:
    (i) drama grade and exam score,   **(ii)** price and preference.

Test yourself ANSWERS

1 (a) Spearman's;   **(b)** PMCC.

2 (a) B/E both equal preferences. The rank values 2 and 3 are shared between them;   **(b)** 0.739 (or 0.741 using $\sum d^2$);   **(c)** Reasonable agreement between preference and price.

3 Non-linear relationship. Data closely connected in rank order but not following a straight line relationship.

4 (a)

Pupil	1	2	3	4	5	6
Drama	2	1	4	5	3	6
Exam	2	1	5	4	3	6

(b)

Cake	1	2	3	4	5	6
Price	4	6	3	2	1	5
Pref	4	1	5	2	6	3

5 (a) 0.943;   **(b)** −0.371;

(c) $H_0 \rho_s = 0$, $H_1 \rho_s \neq 0$, $n = 6$;

(i) ts = 0.943,   cv = 0.8286,   5%; Drama/exam. Reject H_0 significant evidence of association.

(ii) ts = −0.371,   Price/pref: Accept H_0.

CHAPTER 4

Non-parametric hypothesis tests – single sample

4

Learning objectives

After studying this chapter you should be able to:

- understand what is meant by a non-parametric test
- carry out a sign test to test a hypothesis about a population median
- carry out a Wilcoxon signed-rank test to test a hypothesis about a population median.

4.1 The sign test

This is a very simple hypothesis test which requires no knowledge of the distribution of the population from which the sample is taken.

Many tests require that the population involved is known, or assumed, to be normally distributed.

Tests which do not require the knowledge or assumption that the data involved is normally distributed are known as **non-parametric** or **distribution-free tests**.

Non-parametric tests can be used when the data is measured on a ratio scale, such as height or weight. They can also be used when only ordinal (rank order) values are available. For the sign test, all that is needed is to be able to decide whether a particular observation is bigger or smaller than another.

A worked example of a sign test is given below and the technical terms involved in hypothesis testing are explained in the context of this example.

The **sign test** involves allocating a + or − sign to each reading and using a binomial model with $p = \frac{1}{2}$ to determine the critical region.

Sign tests can involve testing whether the median of a population takes a specific value, or, in some cases, for preferences or differences between populations (see Worked example 4.2 and Section 5.4).

Worked example 4.1

The lifetime (hours) of a random sample of ten Xtralong lightbulbs taken from a large batch produced in a factory after an expensive machinery overhaul were:

523, 556, 678, 429, 558, 498, 399, 515, 555, 699

Before the overhaul, the median lifetime of Xtralong bulbs was 500 hours.
Use a sign test, at the 5% **significance level**, to test the hypothesis that the median length of life of Xtralong lightbulbs after the overhaul is greater than 500 hours.

The **significance level** is the level of overwhelming evidence deemed necessary for the decision to conclude that H_0 is not true. It is the probability of wrongly rejecting a true H_0. The smaller the significance level, the more overwhelming the evidence.

Solution

H_0 Population median $= 500$
H_1 Population median > 500

One-tailed test significance level 5%.

If H_0 is true, then

$$P(\text{lifetime} > 500) = P(\text{lifetime} < 500) = \tfrac{1}{2}$$

We are interested in whether a lifetime is recorded as greater or less than 500 hours.

We have a sample of 10 lifetimes, so, if H_0 is true then the number of lifetimes greater than 500 hours should follow a B(10, 0.5) distribution.

A lifetime greater than 500 hours, will be given a $+$ sign and one less than 500 hours, a $-$ sign as follows:

523, 556, 678, 429, 558, 498, 399, 515, 555, 699
$+$ $+$ $+$ $-$ $+$ $-$ $-$ $+$ $+$ $+$

The cumulative binomial tables will normally provide the probabilities necessary to determine the **critical region**, at the **5% level**, for this test.

Note: H_0 must contain $=$ for the sign (or any other) test to be carried out.

If we assume that the median $=$ 500 hours, then half of the population should have a lifetime above 500 and half below 500.

The binomial distribution is being used as a model to enable a test to be carried out.

The use of the $+$ and $-$ is the reason for the test being called the **sign** test.

The **critical region** is the range of values which is so unlikely (with probability 0.05 or less since the **significance level** is 5%) to occur that it will lead to the conclusion that H_0 is not true.

P(0 'more than 500') $= 0.0010$
P(1 or fewer 'more than 500') $= 0.0107$
P(2 or fewer 'more than 500') $= 0.0547$.

The number of positive differences possible out of a sample of 10 readings are:

0,   1,   2,   3,   4,   5,   6,   7,   8,   9,   10

In order to identify the **critical region**, we must identify those extreme outcomes which occur 5% of the time **or less**, assuming H_0 true, $p = \tfrac{1}{2}$.
In other words, the probability of these outcomes must be $\leqslant 0.05$.

Since the probability of a $+$ is 0.5, we also know, by symmetry, that P(0 'more') $=$ P(10 'more')
P(0 or 1 'more') $=$ P(9 or 10 'more')
Hence:
P(10 'more than 500') $= 0.0010$
P(9 or 10 'more than 500') $= 0.0107$
P(8, 9 or 10 'more than 500') $= 0.0547$ and so on.

Note that the number of negative differences will also follow B(10, 0.5).

Since the test is **one-tailed**, only extremely large numbers of positive differences (very small numbers of negative differences) out of the sample of ten need to be considered. The **critical region** will identify the extreme outcomes where high numbers of + signs would occur 5% of the time or less if H_0 is true:

$$0, \quad 1, \quad 2, \quad 3, \quad 4, \quad 5, \quad 6, \quad 7, \quad 8, \quad [9, \quad 10$$
$$* \qquad\qquad P(9, 10) = 0.0107$$

The **critical region** is (9, 10).

> The extreme outcome '9 or 10+' has probability **below** 0.05. The outcome '8, 9 or 10+' has probability close to but **above** 0.05. Using the cumulative binomial tables which provide exact probabilities correct to 4 dp, these two facts identify the **critical region** for this test at a 5% **significance level**.

The **test statistic** for this test is 7+ (or 3−) which is the number of + (or −) signs obtained.
This is labelled * above.

> The **test statistic** is a number found from the sample data assuming that H_0 is true.

It is clear that the **test statistic** does not lie in the extreme **critical region** and therefore we have no **significant** evidence to doubt that H_0 is true.

> Note that this is **not** the same as saying that we have **proved** H_0 is true.

Conclusion

No **significant** evidence at **5% level** to doubt H_0 that the median is 500 hours.

Alternative solution

In the solution to Worked example 4.1, the test statistic was shown to be 7. Therefore, simply noting that $p = P(\geqslant 7+) = 0.1719$, which is considerably greater than 0.05, for this **one-tailed** test, tells us that the test statistic cannot lie in the **critical region** when a 5% **significance level** is used. There is **no significant** evidence to doubt that H_0 is true.
This method makes the calculations involved in carrying out a sign test more straightforward and is recommended in the exam.
If the relevant p value is **greater** than 0.05, accept H_0.
If the relevant p value is **less** than or equal to 0.05, reject H_0.

> This **alternative** method is probably easier and more informative for the sign test. However, for most other distribution-free tests, calculating the p value is much more complex. Instead you will have to use critical values which can be found directly from tables.

> A simpler way to carry out a sign test is to examine the probability, p, of obtaining the test statistic or a more extreme value. If p is smaller than or equal to the stated significance level, then H_0 is rejected. Otherwise, H_0 is accepted.

Worked example 4.2

A random sample of 20 children are asked whether they prefer 'Own Brand' (X) or 'Big Name' (Y) breakfast cereal. Their preferences were:

Y,X,Y,Y,Y,X,Y,Y,Y,Y,Y,Y,Y,X,Y,Y,Y,Y,Y

Use a sign test, at the 1% significance level, to test the hypothesis that children prefer 'Big Name' breakfast cereal.

Solution

H_0 The two breakfast cereals are equally desirable
H_1 'Big Name' is preferred

One-tailed test significance level 1%.

If H_0 is true, then

P('Own Brand' chosen) = P('Big Brand' chosen)
P(X chosen) = P(Y chosen) = $\frac{1}{2}$

We are interested in whether a preference is recorded for Y, which will be indicated +, or for X, indicated −. For the sample of 20 children, if H_0 is true, then the number of + preferences for Y should follow a B(20, 0.5) distribution.

The number of + preferences for Y and − for X are:

Y, X, Y, Y, Y, X, Y, Y, Y, Y, Y, Y, Y, Y, X, Y, Y, Y, Y, Y
+ − + + + − + + + + + + + + − + + + + +

Again, the cumulative binomial tables will provide the probabilities necessary to determine the **critical region**, at the **1% level**, for this test.

P(4 or fewer 'prefer Y') = P(16 or more 'prefer Y') = 0.0059
P(5 or fewer 'prefer Y') = P(15 or more 'prefer Y') = 0.0207.

The number of + signs possible out of a sample of 20 readings are:

0,1,2,3,4,5,6,7,8,9,10,11,12,13,14,15,16,17,18,19,20

In order to identify the **critical region**, we must identify the extreme outcome where high numbers of + occur 1% of the time or less.

The probability of the extremely high number of + must be ≤ 0.01.

0,1,2,3,4,5,6,7,8,9,10,11,12,13,14,15,[16,17,18,19,20
                                                     *

      P($\geq$16+) = 0.0059
but P($\geq$15+) = 0.0207

The **critical region** is (16,17,18,19,20+) because P($\geq$16+) is **less** than 0.01 but P($\geq$15+) **exceeds** 0.01.

The **test statistic** for this test is 17+ (or 3−).
This is labelled * above.

It is clear that the **test statistic** does lie inside the **critical region** and therefore we have overwhelming evidence that H_0 is untrue.

Conclusion

There is **significant** evidence at **1% level** to doubt H_0 that the cereals are equally desirable. We conclude that 'Big Name' is more desirable to children than 'Own Brand' cereal.

Alternative solution

In this example, the test statistic was shown to be 17 and so, noting that $p = P(\geqslant 17+) = 0.0013$ which is considerably **smaller** than 0.01 for this **one-tailed** test, tells us that the test statistic must lie in the **critical region** using a 1% significance level. There is **significant** evidence to reject H_0.

> It is perfectly acceptable to use this alternative method in the exam.

Worked example 4.3

Twenty-one students at a large college undergo a standard test to measure their reaction time to a particular stimulus. The median reaction time in the population generally is believed to be 7.8 seconds.

The reaction times for this sample are:

6.6	3.6	2.1	13.2	5.4	11.6	1.6
7.2	7.8	3.8	6.0	14.2	3.0	15.2
4.7	2.8	7.5	6.9	21.6	6.7	4.3

Use a sign test to test, at the 5% significance level, the hypothesis that the median reaction time is 7.8 seconds.

Solution

H_0 Median reaction time of college students is 7.8 seconds
   Population median = 7.8 seconds
H_1 Median reaction times of students differs from 7.8 seconds
   Population median ≠ 7.8 seconds

Two-tailed test significance level 5%.

If H_0 is true, the

$$P(\text{reaction time} > 7.8) = P(\text{reaction time} < 7.8) = \tfrac{1}{2}$$

We only need consider whether a reaction time is recorded as higher than or lower than 7.8 seconds and so the effective sample size involved is 20 since the subject with reaction time 7.8 seconds cannot be included.

A time above 7.8 is given a + sign, one below a − sign.

If H_0 is true, the number of + signs should follow a B(20, 0.5) distribution.

> Providing the proportion of people recording a reaction time of exactly 7.8 seconds is small, the assumption that, if H_0 is true, P(reaction time > 7.8) = P(reaction time < 7.8) = $\tfrac{1}{2}$ will still be reasonable.

6.6−	3.6−	2.1−	13.2+	5.4−	11.6+	1.6−
7.2−	7.8 .	3.8−	6.0−	14.2+	3.0−	15.2+
4.7−	2.8−	7.5−	6.9−	21.6+	6.7−	4.3−

There are five + signs and 15 − signs.

Cumulative binomial tables again provide the probabilities necessary to determine the **critical region**, at the **5% level** for this test.

As this is a **two-tailed** test, those combined extreme outcomes which occur with probability 0.05 or less must be identified.

> Very large and very small numbers of + (or −) signs are both equally relevant for a two-tailed test.

Considering probabilities of extremes,
P(4 or fewer +) = P(16 or more +) = 0.0059
P(5 or fewer +) = P(15 or more +) = 0.0207
P(6 or fewer +) = P(14 or more +) = 0.0577

The number of + signs possible out of a sample of 20 readings are:

0,1,2,3,4,5,6,7,8,9,10,11,12,13,14,15,16,17,18,19,20

Since the test is **two-tailed**, extremely large or small numbers of + signs must both be included and the **critical region** will consider both these extremes combined together.

0,1,2,3,4,5],6,7,8,9,10,11,12,13,14,[15,16,17,18,19,20+
                                         *

P(≤5) = 0.0207	P(≥15) = 0.0207
P(≤6) = 0.0577	P(≥14) = 0.0577

> Each extreme probability will be doubled when **both** extremes are considered for a **two-tailed** test
>
> 0.0207 + 0.0207 = 0.0414, etc.

The **critical region** is (0,1,2,3,4,5,15,16,17,18,19,20+) because P(≥15) and P(≤5) = 0.0414 combined together which is **less** than 0.05, but P(≥14) and P(≤6) = 0.1154 combined together which **exceeds** 0.05.

The **test statistic** is 15+ (or 5−) which is labelled *.

It is clear that the **test statistic** does lie inside the **critical region** and therefore we have evidence to suggest that H_0 is untrue.

Conclusion

There is **significant** evidence at **5% level** to doubt H_0 that the median reaction time is 7.8 seconds. We therefore conclude that the median reaction time of the population from which this sample was taken differs from 7.8 seconds.

> In this case, because there were a large number of − signs, we think it is very likely that the median reaction time of students is **less** than 7.8 seconds.

Alternative solution

The test statistic is 15 and, noting that $p = P(≥15+) + P(≤5+)$ = 0.0414 for this **two-tailed** test, which is **smaller** than 0.05, this indicates that there is **significant** evidence to reject H_0.

> Both extremes together must be considered for two-tailed tests.

For a **two-tailed** test, it is sufficient to note that that P(≥15+) is less than 0.025 as the 5% significance level can be divided into 2.5% or 0.025 in each tail.

EXERCISE 4A

1 A factory produces lengths of rope for use in boatyards. The breaking strength in kilograms for a random sample of 14 lengths of rope were as follows:

134, 136, 139, 143, 136, 129, 137,
130, 138, 134, 145, 141, 136, 139.

Test the hypothesis that the median breaking strength of all the ropes is 135 kg against the manufacturer's claim that the median breaking strength is greater than 135 kg.
Use the sign test with a 5% level of significance.

2 Twenty-five subjects undergoing a test in a controlled laboratory experiment were recorded as having the following reaction times (seconds) to a particular stimulus:

> 6.5, 3.4, 5.6, 6.9, 7.1, 4.9, 12.9, 7.8, 2.4, 2.8, 15.3, 3.7, 7.8,
> 2.4, 2.8, 3.7, 4.9, 14.0, 6.5, 22.8, 6.9, 7.4, 3.1, 1.9, 19.5

Carry out a sign test at the 5% significance level, to test the hypothesis that the median reaction time for the population from which the subjects were drawn is 7.5 seconds.

3 A psychologist carried out an experiment to find how many six letter words 24 randomly chosen students can recall from a list of 20 such words.
The results were:

12	14	15	8	7	10
11	15	17	18	14	15
7	9	10	11	13	13
15	16	12	14	8	12

From previous experiments, it is known that the median number remembered for the population as a whole is 15. Test at the 1% significance level, the hypothesis that students have a lower median recall value than the population as a whole. Use a sign test.

4 A maze is devised and, after many trials on adult participants, it is found that the median length of time to solve the maze is 7.4 seconds.
A group of nine children was then asked to attempt the maze and their times to completion were:

> 6.1, 9.0, 8.3, 9.4, 5.8, 8.1, 7.6, 9.2, 10.0 seconds

Use a sign test, at the 5% significance level, to test the hypothesis that children take longer to do the maze than adults.

5 A company devises a trial to determine whether members of the public prefer a sunflower oil based spread to one based on olive oil.

Out of the 30 people involved in this trial, only 10 preferred the olive oil based spread, the rest preferring the sunflower oil spread.

Carry out a sign test, at the 5% level, to determine whether there is a significant difference in the popularity of the two types of oil.

*6 An ice cream manufacturer is considering introducing a new flavour cornet and asks a panel of 21 tasters for their opinion of the flavour. The scores were given out of a maximum of 100.

Taster	Score	Taster	Score
A	88	L	51
B	94	M	47
C	79	N	33
D	56	O	55
E	67	P	68
F	53	Q	83
G	66	R	62
H	79	S	61
I	83	T	78
J	59	U	90
K	76		

(a) The median flavour score given by all tasters for the original cornet was 52.
Carry out a sign test at the 1% significance level to determine whether the tasters prefer the new flavour to the original flavour;

(b) If you had been asked to test whether the original flavour was preferred to the new flavour, explain why you would not have needed to use the binomial distribution. [A]

*7 A motoring correspondent assesses the relative merits of two similarly-priced cars, *A* and *B*, by comparing 32 common features. Her results reveal 21 '+ signs' indicating these features are better on *A*, nine '− signs' indicating these features are better on *B*, and two 'zeros' indicating no difference.

(a) Use binomial tables to investigate at the 5% level of significance, the claim that *A* is the better car;

(b) State **two** assumptions that you have made in reaching your conclusion in part **(a)**. [A]

4.2 Wilcoxon signed-rank test

As with the sign test, the Wilcoxon signed-rank test is a distribution-free or non-parametric test where it is not necessary to know or be able to assume that the data involved is normally distributed. However, the Wilcoxon signed-rank test does need the assumption that the population from which the sample is taken is symmetrically distributed and it can only be used for numerical data.

The Wilcoxon signed-rank test is used to test a hypothesis concerning the mean or the median of a population by considering a single sample.

Unlike the sign test which only considers the signs of the differences between the items in the sample and the suggested value of the population median, the Wilcoxon signed-rank test takes into account the size of these differences and puts them in **rank order**. The Wilcoxon test allows, for example, relatively **few** but very **large** + differences to balance many relatively small − differences. It is therefore to be preferred to the sign test.

> Since the population must be symmetrical the mean and the median will be equal.

> The **Wilcoxon signed-rank test** examines the signed differences between each reading and the suggested population mean or median. Rank order values are then assigned to the differences and, for a two-tailed test, the smaller of the totals T+ or T− is the test statistic to be compared with the critical value given in Table 10.

> The **Wilcoxon signed-rank test** requires a symmetric distribution.

> The **Wilcoxon signed-rank test** takes the relative magnitudes of the differences into account and is therefore preferred to the **sign test** provided numerical differences can be obtained.

The easiest way to explain the procedures involved is to work through an example.

Worked example 4.4

The median lifetime of a certain brand of battery is claimed to be 300 hours.
A random sample of 15 of these batteries is taken and their lifetimes recorded:

342	278	302
393	265	289
257	216	312
339	402	249
306	190	178

Use a Wilcoxon signed-rank test, at the 5% significance level, to test whether the claim that the median is 300 hours is justified.

Solution

H_0 Population median $= 300$
H_1 Population median $\neq 300$

Two-tailed test significance level 5%.

The first step in carrying out a Wilcoxon test is to find the signed differences between the given data and 300. These are given in the first column of the following table.

Difference	Rank value +	Rank value −
$+42$	8	
-22		5
$+2$	1	
$+93$	12	
-35		6
-11		3
-43		9
-84		11
$+12$	4	
$+39$	7	
$+102$	13	
-51		10
$+6$	2	
-110		14
-122		15
Totals	$T^+ = 47$	$T^- = 73$

The differences are found for each figure proceeding along the rows of the original data.

The value of the differences are replaced with a **rank order value**. The smallest **absolute difference** is given rank order value 1, the next smallest 2 and so on until the largest difference from the above sample, with 15 valid readings, is given the final rank order value 15.

The number of differences, $n = 15$.

The rank values are grouped as either + or − differences and the totals T^+ and T^- are calculated. where T^+ is the total of the ranks assigned to positive differences and T^- is the total of the ranks assigned to negative differences.

A check can be made on the totals since $T^+ + T^- = \frac{1}{2}n(n+1)$. In this case $47 + 73 = 120$ and $\frac{1}{2}n(n+1) = \frac{1}{2}(15)(16) = 120$.

In this example, $T^+ = 47$ and $T^- = 73$.

In the sign test you were able to calculate the probability of the different outcomes and to deduce the critical region. This is possible but is much more complex for Wilcoxon's test. Fortunately the critical values have been tabulated. Table 10 provides lower tail critical values of the test statistic T. The critical values are given for one- or two-tailed tests and for several significance levels.

It is possible, but unnecessary, to derive the upper tail critical values from Table 10. If T is above the critical value in Table 10, then both T^+ and T^- will lie between the upper and lower critical values.

As Table 10 provides **lower** tail critical values, the procedure for carrying out a two-tailed test is to compare T, the smaller of T^+ and T^-, with the value in Table 10.

The relevant critical value for a two-tailed test with $n = 15$ readings, at the 5% level of significance, is 25.

Therefore, if $T \leqslant 25$, there is significant evidence of a very extreme result which would lead to H_0 being rejected. For this test T is **greater** than 25.

Conclusion

T is **greater** than the critical value so there is no significant evidence at the 5% level to reject H_0 that the median lifetime of batteries is 300 hours

> As you have seen in the sign test, a significance level of exactly, say, 5% cannot usually be obtained. The value shown in Table 10 gives a value as close as possible to that tabulated. Thus the significance level of this critical value may be a little higher or a little lower than 5%. This has no effect on the way the tables are used.

Worked example 4.5

Eleven job applicants are randomly chosen from a large group and asked to attend an interview during which each applicant takes an aptitude test to identify which would be best suited to the job available. The mean score on this test nationally is known to be 64.

The scores of the most recent applicants were:

56, 57, 63, 64, 62, 65, 56, 65, 69, 60, 61

Test the hypothesis, using a 5% significance level, that this group of applicants have a lower aptitude than that found nationally.

Solution

H_0 Mean score in group $= 64$
H_1 Mean score in group < 64

One-tailed test significance level 5%.

Difference	Rank value +	Rank value −
−8		9.5
−7		8
−1		2
0	discard	
−2		4
+1	2	
−8		9.5
+1	2	
+5	7	
−4		6
−3		5
Totals	$T^+ = 11$	$T^- = 44$

> Differences equal to zero must be discarded. This will affect the calculation of the critical values. However, provided only a small proportion of observations are discarded, Table 10 can still be used to find critical values.

In this example, some of the absolute differences are the same. The individual rank values 1, 2, 3, ..., 10 cannot be assigned in the usual way and the rule is that to each of the equal differences, the **average** of the ranks they would normally have received is assigned.

> This is the same method you used for Spearman's rank correlation coefficient.

The absolute difference 1 occurs three times and those three places should have been allocated the ranks 1, 2 and 3.

The average is $\dfrac{1+2+3}{3} = 2$ so all receive rank 2.

The absolute difference 8 occurs twice and those 2 places should have been allocated the ranks 9 and 10.
The average of these two ranks is 9.5 so each receives rank 9.5.

In this example, the alternative hypothesis, H_1 is mean <64.
If H_1 is true, we would expect T^- to be large and T^+ to be small. As the lower tail is given in Table 10, the procedure is compare T^+ with the critical value in Table 10 to see if it is small enough for us to conclude that H_0 can be rejected and H_1 accepted.

Table 12 gives the **one-tailed** critical value at 5% level as 11.

Therefore if $T^+ \leqslant 11$, there is significant evidence of an extreme result which would lead to H_0 being rejected. For this one-tailed test the test statistic is equal to T^+. That is $T = 11$.

> The **critical region** includes the value given in the table.

Conclusion

T is **equal** to the critical value and therefore there is significant evidence at the 5% level to reject H_0 and conclude that the mean score for the group of applicants is lower than 64.

EXERCISE 4B

1 For the data given in Question **1** of Exercise 4A, test the hypothesis again, this time using the Wilcoxon signed-rank test at the 5% level.

2 For the data given in Question **4** of Exercise 4A, test the hypothesis again, this time using the Wilcoxon signed-rank test at a 5% significance level.

3 The birth rate in an African State is believed to have a mean value of 51 births per year per 1000 population.
After an intensive education programme in one particular area of this state, birth rates in 12 large settlements in this area are recorded as:

> 47.5, 48.8, 47.8, 50.1, 49.0, 52.0,
> 46.0, 50.3, 42.5, 47.0, 43.6, 43.8.

Test whether the mean birth rate seems to have declined in this area using a Wilcoxon signed-rank test at the 1% level of significance.
(Remember that for a Wilcoxon test to be carried out, the population must be symmetrical and hence the mean and median are the same. See Section 4.2.)

4 A Spanish teacher sets her A level students a set of words to learn. This vocabulary list contains 30 words and the median number correct in previous years was 23.

The number of words correctly remembered by a sample of 21 students this year are:

24, 29, 27, 15, 23, 30, 25,
28, 29, 21, 19, 22, 25, 26,
24, 26, 27, 24, 28, 17, 24.

Use a Wilcoxon signed-rank test at the 5% level of significance to determine whether there is evidence that her students this year have achieved a higher median score in the vocabulary test.

5 A random sample of patients visiting a large outpatients clinic at a hospital is asked to record how many times they have visited their General Practitioner during the past year with the following results:

7, 6, 5, 4, 5, 5, 2, 3, 6, 1, 3, 11, 9, 1.

The mean number of visits per year in the local population is believed to be 4. Test the hypothesis, at the 5% level, that the mean number of visits per year for patients visiting outpatients is higher than for people in the local population.

6 The following data relates to the amount of money, to the nearest $, spent by a random sample of 16 visitors to a Theme Park in the USA:

84, 72, 98, 108, 135, 115, 68, 102,
78, 89, 77, 105, 112, 85, 69, 108.

Using the Wilcoxon signed-rank test, test the hypothesis that the median amount spent, per visitor, is $95. Use the 5% significance level.

7 The values below are the scores obtained by a batsman in a random sample of 20 innings in one-day cricket matches.

26, 0, 0, 0, 103,
28, 16, 8, 14, 0
18, 47, 0, 2, 0
52, 25, 128, 26, 84.

The batsman's median score for all innings in four-day cricket matches is 30.

(a) Using a sign test at the 5% level of significance, investigate the claim that the batsman's median score in one-day cricket matches is less than that in four-day matches;

(b) Using a Wilcoxon signed-rank test, also at the 5% significance level, test the same hypothesis.　　　[A]

*8 The median life of a make of candle is 270 minutes.
A different make of candle is claimed to have a median life
longer than 200 minutes.
To test this, 20 of the new candles are lit and after 200
minutes it is observed six have burnt out but the remainder
are still burning.

(a) Use an appropriate non-parametric test to investigate
the claim that the median life exceeds 200 minutes. Use
a 5% significance level.

The six candles which had burnt out lasted

162,   179,   183,   184,   189,   195 minutes.

The next candles to burn out lasted

210,   215,   225,   234 and 239 minutes.

The remaining nine candles were still burning after
240 minutes;

(b) Use Wilcoxon's signed-rank test, at the 1% significance
level, to investigate the claim that the median life of the
new candles exceeds 200 minutes;

(c) State two assumptions it was necessary to make in
order to carry out the test in part **(b)**;

(d) Explain why it would not have been possible to apply
Wilcoxon's signed-rank test when the sample of candles
had been burning for 212 minutes.   [A]

*9 The external diameters (measured in units of 0.01 mm above
a nominal value) of a random sample of piston rings from a
large consignment were:

11,   9,   32,   18,   29,   1,   21,   19,   6,   3.

(a) Use Wilcoxon's signed rank test, at the 5% significance
level, to investigate the claim that the median external
diameter is 20;

It was later discovered that an error had been made in
zeroing the measuring device and that all the measurements
in the sample should be increased by 12.

(b) Repeat part **(a)** using the correct measurements;

A technician carried out the tests in parts **(a)** and **(b)** and in
each case accepted the null hypothesis. She suspected an error
in her calculations because, although the sample median had
increased by 12 in part **(b)** compared to part **(a)**, she had
accepted the same conclusion about the median in both cases.

(c) In the context of this example explain the meaning of
  (i)   null hypothesis,
  (ii) Type 1 error,
  (iii) Type 2 error.

Hence explain to the technician why there is no reason for
her to conclude that there was an error in her calculations.

                                                          [A]

*10 It is claimed that adults in the UK visit the cinema on average more than 12 times per year. A sample of 30 adults in the UK contained 23 who had visited the cinema more than 12 times in the last year and 7 who had visited the cinema less than 12 times in the last year.

(a) Use a suitable non-parametric test to investigate the claim at the 1% significance level;

(b) How would your conclusion be affected if you were given the following pieces of information? Answer each part separately.

(i) The number of cinema visits does not follow a normal distribution,

(ii) The distribution of the number of cinema visits is not symmetrical,

(iii) The data was gathered by interviewing adults as they left a cinema. [A]

*11 For a particular breed of sheep the median weight of new born lambs is believed to be 2.9 kg.
Investigate whether the median weight is:

(a) equal to 2.9 kg if a random sample of 20 new born lambs contains five which weigh over 2.9 kg and 15 which weigh under 2.9 kg. Use a 5% significance level;

(b) at least 2.9 kg if a random sample of 25 new born lambs contains 18 which weigh under 2.9 kg, two which weigh exactly 2.9 kg and five which weigh over 2.9kg. Use a 1% significance level;

(c) not more than 2.9 kg if a random sample of 30 new born lambs contains 21 which weigh under 2.9 kg. Use a 0.1% significance level. [A]

> The weights were recorded to one decimal place which explains why it is possible for two to weigh exactly 2.9 kg.

Key point summary

1 A **distribution-free** or **non-parametric** test does   *p65*
not require the knowledge or assumption that the
data involved is normally distributed.

2 The **sign test** involves allocating a + or − sign to   *p65*
each reading and using a binomial model with $p = \frac{1}{2}$
to determine the critical region. Usually, the
cumulative binomial tables can be used.

3 Alternatively, a sign test can be carried out by examining the relevant probability, p, of obtaining the test statistic or a more extreme value. If p is smaller than the stated significance level, then $\mathbf{H_0}$ is rejected. Otherwise, $\mathbf{H_0}$ is accepted. This is a simpler way to carry out the sign test and is acceptable in the exam. *p67*

4 The **Wilcoxon signed-rank test** examines the signed differences between each reading and the suggested population mean or median. Rank order values are then assigned to the differences and, for a two-tailed test, the smaller of the totals T^+ or T^- is the test statistic to be compared with the critical value given in Table 10. If there are 'tied ranks' or equal differences, then the average of the relevant rank values is applied to each reading. *p73*

5 The **Wilcoxon signed-rank test** requires a symmetrical distribution. *p73*

6 The **Wilcoxon signed-rank test** takes the relative magnitudes of the differences into account and is therefore preferred to the **sign test** provided numerical differences can be obtained. *p73*

Test yourself	What to review
1 What is the name of the type of hypothesis tests for which it is not necessary to assume that the data are normally distributed?	*Section 4.1*
2 Give a reason why the Wilcoxon signed-rank test may be better to use than the sign test, to test whether a population median takes a particular value.	*Section 4.2*
3 Which non-parametric test can be used when the data involved is not numerical?	*Section 4.1*
4 For the single sample sign test for a population median, what value of p is used in the binomial model $B(n, p)$?	*Section 4.1*
5 A sign test is carried out on a sample with 14 valid readings. The sign $+$ is allocated to readings above the suggested median for the population and the sign $-$ to those below this median value. Find the critical region for: **(a)** a two-tailed test at 5% significance level; **(b)** a one-tailed test, looking for an increase, at 5% significance level; **(c)** a two-tailed test at the 1% significance level.	*Section 4.1*

Test yourself (*continued*) | **What to review**

6 In a Wilcoxon signed-rank test, the following signed differences *Section 4.2*
are obtained:

$$-4, \quad 6, \quad -2, \quad 1.5, \quad -4, \quad -3, \quad 3, \quad 5, \quad 6, \quad 4, \quad 0.5, \quad 7.$$

Give the signed-rank values which would be allocated to the
differences above.

---

7 In a survey of rush-hour motorists, the distances, in km, *Sections 4.1 and 4.2*
travelled to work by a random sample of motorists, who
were travelling alone, were:

$$14, \quad 43, \quad 17, \quad 52, \quad 8, \quad 22, \quad 25, \quad 68, \quad 32, \quad 26, \quad 44.$$

Test the hypothesis, at the 5% significance level, that the
median distance travelled to work by motorists
travelling alone is 25 km, using:

(a) the sign test;

(b) the Wilcoxon signed-rank test.

Comment on your results.

4

Test yourself ANSWERS

1 Non-parametric.

2 Takes into account rank order of differences – not just the sign of the
differences.

3 Sign test.

4 $p = 0.5$.

5 (a) $\{0,1,2,12,13,14\}$ probability < 0.05 [$\{0,1,2,3,11,12,13,14\}$ has probability
closest to 5%, 0.05 (but bigger)];

(b) $\{11,12,13,14\}$;

(c) $\{0,1,13,14\}$ probability < 0.01 [$\{0,1,2,12,13,14\}$ has probability closest to
1%, 0.01 (but bigger)].

6 $-7, +10\frac{1}{2}, -3, +2, -7, -4\frac{1}{2}, +4\frac{1}{2}, +9, +10\frac{1}{2}, +7, +1, +12.$

7 (a) H_0 med $= 25$, H_1 med $\neq 25$, ts $= 6^+$ or 4^- $n = 10$,   5% two-tail.
$P(\geqslant 6^+) = P(\leqslant 4^-) = 0.377 > 2.5\%$.
Accept H_0 No significant evidence to doubt med $= 25$.

(b) H_0 med $= 25$, H_1 med $\neq 25$, $T^+ = 38, T^- = 17$,   5% two-tail.
$n = 10$,   cv $= 8$,   ts $= 17$.
Accept H_0 No significant evidence to doubt med $= 25$.
In this case both tests lead to the same conclusion.

CHAPTER 5

Simple experimental design and paired tests

Learning objectives

After studying this chapter you should be able to:

■ understand what is meant by control and experimental groups
■ appreciate why blind and double blind trials are used
■ understand the meaning of experimental error, bias and replication
■ carry out a non-parametric sign test or Wilcoxon signed-rank test on paired data.

5.1 Control and experimental groups

When the effect of just one experimental treatment is to be tested, it is necessary to ensure that a **baseline** measure is taken so that data is available to compare with the performance of the treatment. For example, if a new drug, intended to alleviate the symptoms of arthritis sufferers, is to be tested, it would be quite unsatisfactory to simply take a group of sufferers and give them the drug and note how many of them improved. An arthritis sufferer may improve (or deteriorate) over a period of time with no treatment at all. It is clearly essential to have two, similarly matched groups: one, the control group, is chosen at random to receive no treatment or to continue with the standard treatment for arthritis and the other, the **experimental group**, will receive the new drug. The effects on the two groups can then be compared.

> These two groups need to be matched as closely as possible. For example, the arthritis sufferers in the **control** group should overall match those in the **experimental** group in terms of age, general health, gender and severity of arthritis.

> To test the effect of one experimental treatment, a **control group**, which receives no active treatment or the standard treatment, and an **experimental group**, which receives the new treatment, are used.

5.2 Blind and double blind trials

In the case of medical treatment, as in the example above, it is sometimes thought that patients will improve or recover without treatment at all and that, in some cases, this improvement will be greater or quicker if they think they are getting a new treatment, even if they are not. Therefore, it is standard practice in trials of new drugs to carry out a **blind trial** in which patients do not know whether they are in the **control** or the **experimental** group. In order for this to work, patients in the **control** group are given a **placebo** which is a harmless substance that looks like the real new medication but does not in fact contain the new drug at all. Trials in which patients do not know whether they are taking a placebo or a new drug are called **blind trials**.

> A **placebo** or non-active substance is often given to the **control group** in an experimental trial.

Quite complex effects can be at work in drug trials. It often happens that, even if patients are unaware of whether they are taking the new drug or the **placebo**, the medical staff dealing with the patients may expect those taking the new drug to show greater improvement than those taking the **placebo**. Therefore, the staff might talk differently to the patients on the new drug and transmit to them, in a subtle way, the expectation that they are improving. It is desirable then that the medical staff also do not know which patients are taking the new drug and which the **placebo**. Trials where neither the patient nor the medical staff in direct contact with them know who is receiving the drugs are called **double blind** trials.

Sometimes, **blind** or **double blind** trials are not possible because of *ethical* problems which arise. For example, if there was a strong likelihood of adverse side effects from a new treatment, then the patient would have to be informed of this and the medical staff may need to monitor those receiving the new treatment differently.

> **Blind** and **double blind** trials are used to ensure that results are not influenced by expectations of the subject involved or the staff looking after the subject, that a new treatment will lead to greater improvement or will cause side effects of a particular type.

5.3 Experimental design

Variability of experimental results is a fact of life and something we all expect. You may well, when at school, have been given a seed from a sunflower to plant. Everybody had similar sized seeds from the same flower and you all planted them in identical pots supplied by your teacher. They had the same conditions to grow and yet nobody would expect them all to grow to exactly the same height. Indeed, the fun of this trial was often to see whose seed grew into the tallest plant. Such variability of results is called **experimental error** which does not mean that a mistake has been made but rather that there are always other factors affecting results. In this case, some seeds were probably 'stronger' than others, some seeds were slightly

To try to show that a new drug is effective or to show it is more effective than a standard treatment, significantly more patients who took the drug must show an improvement than those who took the **placebo**.

Clearly, the pharmacist who is dispensing the drugs would have to know which patient is in which group. This pharmacist would not meet the patients and would ensure that both groups received drugs which appeared identical to look at.

Blind and double blind trials are not specifically in the S3 specification. They have been included here for completeness and because the idea of bias may be tested. Questions such as 'What is a blind trial?' will not be asked in S3.

Questions on Experimental design will occur in Exercise 5A and Exercise 5B.

over- or under-watered etc. and some pots were at the sunny end of the windowsill, others were not. **Experimental error** should be minimised by keeping factors which are not being investigated as constant as possible and by careful experimental design.

What factors could be kept constant in an experiment to compare the petrol consumption of two different makes of car?
There are many factors to consider, such as:
same driver used, same route taken, same time of day for trials, same brand of fuel used, same weather conditions.

It is desirable to take **repeated observations** or **replicates** under apparently identical conditions in order to estimate the **experimental error**. In the previous example, if the fuel consumption of a make of car is estimated several times these are **replicates**. If these estimates are made by the same driver, taking the same route, using the same fuel, at the same time of day in the same weather conditions (as far as is feasible), then the **experimental error** will be reduced.

> The purpose of having **replicates** is to estimate the magnitude of the experimental error because the only possible differences would be due to experimental error not due to the factors being investigated.

One of the simplest experimental designs which is often used to reduce **experimental error** is to plan **paired comparisons**. For example, if the response times of school pupils to a particular stimulus are believed to be faster before 10 am than after 4 pm, one group of 30 pupils could be tested at 9.30 am and another group at 4.30 pm. However, the fact that pupils are known to vary enormously in their response times, means that it becomes difficult to determine if differences between the groups really are due to the time of day or due to the inbuilt differences between the two groups. A far better design would be to use the same 30 pupils for both tests and then any difference could be attributed to the time of day since no variability between the pupils exists: they are the same pupils!

> You will meet two examples of non-parametric tests for analysing paired comparisons later in this chapter: the sign and the Wilcoxon signed-rank test.

Similarly, to compare weight loss due to two different slimming diets, an ideal design would be to secure the cooperation of several pairs of identical twins of similar weights. One twin of each pair would follow one diet and the other twin the second diet. Then, any **experimental error** due to physiological differences in the people following the two diets would be minimised.

> **Experimental design** is used to eliminate **bias** and reduce **experimental error** in data collection.

5.4 The paired sample sign test

The sign test which was introduced in Chapter 4 can easily be adapted to test for a difference between paired samples. In the slimming example mentioned above, the aim is to establish which (if either) diet leads to the greater weight loss on average. In order to carry out the sign test, this has to be formulated more

> If a paired test is not possible then a test on two **separate** samples of data is the only option. Chapter 6 introduces the Mann–Whitney U test which is the non-parametric test used in this situation.

precisely. The **H₀** used this time is that the differences between the pairs come from a population which has median equal to zero. Under this **H₀**, the second reading in each pair is equally likely to be greater than or smaller than the first. This is exactly the same situation as in the single sample sign test seen in Chapter 4. An example will explain how this works.

> A **paired comparison** is a simple experimental design which can be used to reduce experimental error when two treatments are being compared.

Worked example 5.1

To measure the effectiveness of a drug for asthmatic relief, 12 subjects, all susceptible to asthma, were each administered the drug after one asthma attack and the placebo after a separate asthma attack. One hour after the attack an asthmatic index was obtained on each subject with the following results:

Subject	1	2	3	4	5	6	7	8	9	10	11	12
Drug	28	31	17	18	31	12	33	24	18	25	19	17
Placebo	32	33	23	26	34	17	30	24	19	23	21	24

Making no assumptions regarding the distribution of these data, investigate the claim that the drug significantly reduces the asthmatic index using a sign test at the 5% significance level.

> The use of the word **reduces** indicates that this is a one-tailed test.

Solution

H₀ Population median difference $= 0$
H₁ Population median difference > 0

> Where difference is taken as placebo − drug measure.

One-tailed test significance level 5%.

If **H₀** is true, then, for the index concerned

$$P(\text{placebo} < \text{drug measure}) = P(\text{placebo} > \text{drug measure})$$
$$P(\text{difference} +) = P(\text{difference} -) = \tfrac{1}{2}$$

The differences are given below.
They are all placebo index–drug index

$$+ \ + \ + \ + \ + \ + \ - \ . \ + \ - \ + \ +$$

> It does not matter whether you find differences as placebo − drug, as found here, or as drug − placebo **but** you must be consistent throughout the solution.

There are 11 valid signs as subject 8 scored 24 both times. As before, the cumulative binomial tables will provide the probabilities necessary to determine the critical region, at the 5% level, for this test.
The model used in this case is B(11, 0.5).

> Remember that the sign test requires a + or − sign so a zero difference cannot be included.

The possible number of + signs for this model are:

$$0, \ 1, \ 2, \ 3, \ 4, \ 5, \ 6, \ 7, \ 8, \ [9, \ 10, \ 11+$$
$$*$$

From the tables,

$P(11+) = 0.0005$

$P(10 \text{ or } 11+) = 0.0059$

$P(9, 10 \text{ or } 11+) = 0.0327$

The **test statistic** is the number of + signs obtained, in this case 9 as indicated * above.

Considering the **test statistic**, you can see that $P(\geqslant 9+)$ is 0.0327 which is less than 0.05 and so $\mathbf{H_0}$ is rejected.

Also from the tables, $P(8, 9, 10 \text{ or } 11+) = 0.1133$. This identifies the critical region as $(9, 10, 11+)$ since $P(9, 10 \text{ or } 11+)$ is **less** than 0.05, but $P(8, 9, 10 \text{ or } 11+)$ is **too big** at 5% level. The **test statistic** 9 lies inside the critical region and so we reject $\mathbf{H_0}$.

Conclusion

The test statistic lies in the critical region at the 5% level and so $\mathbf{H_0}$ is rejected and we conclude that there is significant evidence that the drug does reduce the index.

The paired-sample sign test can also be used on non-numerical data as Worked example 5.2 illustrates.

Worked example 5.2

Fifteen girls were each given an oral examination and a written examination in French. Their grades (highest = A, lowest = F) in the two examinations were as follows.

Girl	1	2	3	4	5	6	7	8	9	10	11	12	13	14	15
Oral exam	A	B	C	D	F	C	B	E	E	C	D	C	E	C	B
Written exam	B	D	D	C	E	D	C	D	C	D	E	E	F	D	C

Using the sign test, investigate the hypothesis that one examination produces significantly different grades from the other, using a 5% level of significance.

Solution

$\mathbf{H_0}$ Population median difference = 0

$\mathbf{H_1}$ Population median difference $\neq$ 0

Two-tailed test significance level 5%.

If $\mathbf{H_0}$ is true, then, for the grades,

$P(\text{oral} < \text{written}) = P(\text{oral} > \text{written})$

$P(\text{difference} +) = P(\text{difference} -) = \frac{1}{2}$

The differences, oral − written grade, are given below.

$$+ \quad + \quad + \quad - \quad - \quad + \quad + \quad - \quad - \quad + \quad + \quad + \quad + \quad + \quad +$$

The model used in this case is $B(15, 0.5)$.

The possible number of + signs for this model are:

$$0, \ 1, \ 2, \ 3,] \ 4, \ 5, \ 6, \ 7, \ 8, \ 9, \ 10, \ 11, \ [12, \ 13, \ 14, \ 15+$$
$$*$$

The **test statistic** is the number of + signs obtained, in this case 11 as indicated * above.

Noting that $P(\geqslant 11+)$ together with $P(\leqslant 4+)$, for this two-tailed test, is 0.1184 which is **greater** than 0.05 leads to the conclusion that there is no significance evidence to reject $\mathbf{H_0}$.

From the tables:

$P(0, 1, 2, 3+) = 0.0176$

$= P(12, 13, 14, 15+)$

This identifies the critical region, considering both extremes together for this **two-tailed** test, as:

$(0, 1, 2, 3, 12, 13, 14, 15+)$

since the **combined** probability for this event is

$0.0176 + 0.0176 = 0.0352$

which is less than 0.05.

However, $P(0, 1, 2, 3, 4+)$

$= 0.05925 = P(11, 12, 13, 14$ or $15+)$ which combined gives a total probability of 0.1184 which is **too big** at the 5% level.

Conclusion

The test statistic does not lie in the critical region so there is no significant evidence to doubt H_0. No significant difference in grades found.

The test statistic 11 does **not** lie in the critical region and so you can accept H_0.

EXERCISE 5A

1 Ten athletes ran a fixed 200 m distance on successive days, firstly on a synthetic athletic track and then on a conventional cinder track. The decision whether each athlete ran on cinder first or synthetic first was made at random. The results in seconds were as follows:

Athlete	1	2	3	4	5	6	7	8	9	10
Synthetic	26.5	25.8	27.2	28.1	25.6	25.5	28.8	27.1	24.1	26.6
Cinder	26.6	26.1	27.4	28.0	25.8	26.6	29.1	27.0	24.8	26.8

Carry out a sign test, at the 5% significance level, to determine whether the nature of the surface influences athletes' performance in the 200 m.

2 Ten psychology students carried out an experiment. They wished to test whether the ability to perform a simple control task is influenced by the presence of an audience.

Each student carried out the task on their own first and measured the time taken. Then, each student performed the same task again in front of an audience. The time results (seconds) were:

Student	A	B	C	D	E	F	G	H	I	J
Alone	45.4	48.2	47.5	49.1	54.3	45.5	58.2	47.1	54.3	46.8
Audience	46.7	51.2	47.8	48.0	55.8	46.6	59.1	47.0	54.8	49.6

(a) Explain why this is known as a paired test;

(b) Explain how experimental error is reduced by using paired data;

(c) Carry out a sign test at the 5% significance level to determine whether students take longer to perform this task when an audience is present;

(d) What problem arises in interpreting the results of this experiment? How could the design have been improved in order to avoid this problem?   [A]

3 Pairs of twins, where each twin suffers from moderate eczema, are recruited for the trial of a new skin preparation. The trial is a double blind trial in which the twin selected at random to be in the control group is given a placebo. The percentage improvement after 4 weeks of treatment was assessed with the following results:

Twin	1	2	3	4	5	6	7	8
Placebo	16	10	16	22	22	24	24	11
New prep	21	16	20	25	20	28	26	15

(a) Explain what is meant by a double blind trial;

(b) Explain what is meant by a placebo;

(c) Carry out a sign test, at the 5% significance level, to determine whether the new preparation appears to result in a twin having a higher percentage improvement of their eczema. [A]

4 Identical programs were run on two different makes of personal computers and the load times (seconds) on each machine, for each program, were noted.

Carry out a non-parametric test on this paired data to determine whether there is any evidence of a difference in load times between the two personal computers. Use the sign test at the 5% level.

Program	1	2	3	4	5	6	7	8	9	10	11	12
PC A	37	77	49	26	23	16	15	11	45	25	9	55
PC B	30	66	47	22	20	14	17	13	43	31	7	41

[A]

5 On the 2nd July 1980 the incoming mail in each of 12 selected towns was randomly divided into two similar lots prior to sorting. In each town one lot was then sorted by the traditional sorting method, the other by a new Electronic Post Code Sensor Device (EPCSD). The times taken, in hours, to complete these jobs are recorded below.

Town	A	B	C	D	E	F	G	H	I	J	K	L
Hand sort time	4.3	4.1	5.6	4.0	5.9	4.9	4.3	5.4	5.6	5.2	6.1	4.7
EPCSD sort time	3.7	5.3	4.5	3.1	4.8	5.0	3.5	4.9	4.6	4.1	5.7	3.5

Use the sign test and a 5% level of significance to test the null hypothesis of no difference in the times against the alternative hypothesis that the EPCSD method is quicker.

What further information would you require before making a decision whether or not to change over to the new EPCSD system? [A]

5.5 The paired sample Wilcoxon signed-rank test

As you can see from Worked example 5.1, the procedure involved in carrying out a paired sign test is exactly the same as that used for a one sample sign test except that the differences between pairs are used. In much the same way, you already know the procedure to follow for the Wilcoxon signed-rank test on paired data. The following example will explain further.

> The **sign test** and the **Wilcoxon signed-rank test** are **non-parametric tests** which can be used to test for differences between **paired** data.

Worked example 5.3

In a comparison of two computerised methods, A and B, for measuring physical fitness, a random sample of eight people were assessed by both methods. Their scores (maximum 20) were recorded as follows.

Subject	1	2	3	4	5	6	7	8
Method A	11.2	8.6	6.5	17.3	14.3	10.7	9.8	13.3
Method B	10.4	12.1	9.1	15.6	16.7	10.7	12.8	15.5

Use a Wilcoxon signed-rank test, at the 5% significance level, to test whether the claim that Method A gives a lower measure of fitness than Method B is justified.

Solution

H_0 Population mean difference $= 0$
H_1 Population mean difference $(A - B) < 0$

One-tailed test significance level 5%.

The first step in carrying out a Wilcoxon test on paired data is to find the signed differences between the pairs.

Difference	Rank value	
(A − B)	**+**	**−**
+0.8	1	
−3.5		7
−2.6		5
+1.7	2	
−2.4		4
0	Discard	
−3.0		6
−2.2		3
Totals	$T^+ = 3$	$T^- = 25$

Any differences equal to zero must be discarded.

As in the previous examples of the Wilcoxon test, the **absolute** value of the remaining differences are replaced with a **rank order value** and these rank values are grouped as either $+$ or $-$ differences. The rank values and their totals T^+ and T^- are given in the previous table.

Since $\mathbf{H_1}$ is that Method A gives a **lower** measure of fitness than Method B, the null hypothesis $\mathbf{H_0}$ will be rejected if T^+ is small. As Table 12 gives the lower critical tail values, it is always advisable to consider which of T^+ and T^- is expected to be small for a one-tail test and then compare this value with the relevant critical value.

The relevant critical value from Table 12 for a one-tailed test with $n = 7$ readings, at the 5% level of significance, is 4.

Therefore, if $T^+ \leq 4$, there is significant evidence of a very extreme result which would lead to $\mathbf{H_0}$ being rejected. For this test $T^+ = 3$.

> You can check your totals
> $T^+ + T^- = \frac{1}{2}n(n + 1)$ always
> $3 + 25 = 28 = \frac{1}{2}7(7 + 1)$

Conclusion

$\mathbf{T^+}$ is less than the critical value so we reject $\mathbf{H_0}$ at the 5% significance level and conclude that there is significant evidence to suggest Method A does give a lower average measure of fitness.

Worked example 5.4

An athletics coach wishes to test the value to athletes of an intensive period of weight training and so selects twelve 400-metre runners from the region and records their times, in seconds, to complete this distance. They then undergo the programme of weight training and have their times, in seconds, for 400 metres measured again. The table below summarises the results.

Athlete	A	B	C	D	E	F	G	H	I	J	K	L
Before	51.0	49.8	49.5	50.1	51.6	48.9	52.4	50.6	53.1	48.6	52.9	53.4
After	50.6	50.4	48.9	49.1	51.6	47.6	53.5	49.9	51.0	48.5	50.6	51.7

Use the Wilcoxon signed-rank test at 5% significance level to investigate the hypothesis that the training programme will significantly improve athletes' times for the 400 metres.

Solution

$\mathbf{H_0}$ Population mean difference $= 0$
$\mathbf{H_1}$ Population mean difference (before $-$ after) > 0

One-tailed test significance level 5%.

> The word *improve* indicates a one-tailed test.

| Difference | Rank value | |
(before − after)	+	−
+0.4	2	
−0.6		3.5
+0.6	3.5	
+1.0	6	
0	Discard	
+1.3	8	
−1.1		7
+0.7	5	
+2.1	10	
+0.1	1	
+2.3	11	
+1.7	9	
Totals	$T^+ = 55.5$	$T^- = 10.5$

5

Since H_1 is that the training programme will reduce the times, we will reject H_0 and accept H_1 if T^- is small.

The relevant critical value from Table 12 for a one-tailed test with $n = 11$ readings, at the 5% level of significance, is 14. Therefore, if $T^- \leqslant 14$, there is significant evidence of a very extreme result which would lead to H_0 being rejected. For this test T^- is 10.5, clearly **less** than 14.

> Again, check the T^+ and T^- with
> $T^+ + T^- = \frac{1}{2}n(n + 1)$
> $55.5 + 10.5 = 66 = \frac{1}{2}11(11 + 1)$

Conclusion

T is less than the critical value so there is significant evidence at the 5% level to reject H_0 and conclude that there is significant evidence to suggest the mean time before is **greater** than the mean time after training. The training programme does appear to significantly improve athletes' times.

Worked example 5.5

As part of her research into the behaviour of the human memory, a psychologist asked 15 schoolgirls to talk for 5 minutes on 'my day at school'. Each girl was then asked to record how many times she thought that she had used the word nice during this period. The table below gives their replies together with the true values.

Girl	A	B	C	D	E	F	G	H	I	J	K	L	M	N	O
True value	12	20	1	8	0	12	12	17	6	5	24	23	10	18	16
Recorded value	9	21	3	14	4	12	16	14	5	9	20	16	11	17	19

Use Wilcoxon's test to investigate whether schoolgirls tend to underestimate or overestimate the frequency with which they use a particular word in a verbal description. Use a 5% significance level.

Solution

H_0 Population mean difference $= 0$
H_1 Population mean difference (true − recorded) $\neq 0$

Two-tailed test significance level 5%.

Difference	Rank value	
(true − recorded)	+	−
+3	7	
−1		2.5
−2		5
−6		13
−4		10.5
0	Discard	
−4		10.5
+3	7	
+1	2.5	
−4		10.5
+4	10.5	
+7	14	
−1		2.5
+1	2.5	
−3		7
Totals	$T^+ = 43.5$	$T^- = 61.5$

The test involved in this example is two-tailed and, since Table 12 provides lower tail critical values, it is only necessary to compare the smaller of T^+ and T^- with the tabulated value.

In this case the test statistic $T = 43.5$ and the two-tailed critical value for a sample of 14 valid differences is 21.

T is above the critical value and so we accept H_0.

Again, check the T^+ and T^- with
$T^+ + T^- = \frac{1}{2}n(n + 1)$
$43.5 + 61.5 = 105 = \frac{1}{2}14(14 + 1)$

Remember from Chapter 4, Section 4.2, that it is not necessary to obtain the upper tail critical value.

If **T** is above the critical value then both T^+ and T^- will lie between the upper and lower critical values.

Conclusion

There is no significant evidence to doubt H_0 and so we conclude that there is no evidence that girls tend either to underestimate or to overestimate the frequency with which they use the word 'nice'.

EXERCISE 5B

1 For the data given in Exercise 5A Question **1**;

   (a) Comment briefly on the experimental design used;

   (b) Carry out a Wilcoxon signed-rank test, at the 5% significance level, to determine whether the nature of the surface influences athletes' performance in the 200 m.

2 Carry out a Wilcoxon signed-rank test on the data given in Exercise 5A Question **2** to investigate whether the median time taken by students to perform the task is greater when an audience is present. Use a 5% significance level.

3 Carry out a Wilcoxon signed-rank test on the data given in Exercise 5A Question **3** to investigate whether the new preparation results in a twin having a higher mean percentage improvement of their eczema. Use a 1% significance level.

4 Identical programs were run on two different makes of personal computers and the load times (seconds) on each machine, for each program, were noted.

Program	1	2	3	4	5	6	7	8	9	10	11	12
PC A	37	77	49	26	23	16	12	12	45	25	10	55
PC B	30	66	47	22	20	14	17	13	43	31	7	41

Use the Wilcoxon signed-rank test, at the 5% significance level, to determine whether there is any evidence of a difference in mean load times between the two personal computers.

5 The blood clotting times for eight people were measured before and after they had consumed a fixed amount of alcohol. The times (seconds) are given below:

Person	1	2	3	4	5	6	7	8
Before	124	167	129	117	146	16	119	149
After	126	117	134	127	126	128	114	99

(a) Comment on the use of a paired design for this experiment;

(b) Test, at the 5% significance level, the hypothesis that the consumption of alcohol has no effect on the median clotting time of blood. Use a Wilcoxon signed-rank test.

6 The Ministry of Defence is considering which of two shoe leathers it should adopt for its new Army boot. They are particularly interested in how boots made from these leathers wear and so 15 soldiers are selected at random and each soldier wears one boot of each type. After six months the wear, in millimetres, for each boot is recorded as follows.

Soldier	1	2	3	4	5	6	7	8	9	10	11	12	13	14	15
Leather A	5.4	2.6	4.3	1.1	3.3	6.6	4.4	3.5	1.2	1.3	4.8	1.2	2.8	2.0	6.1
Leather B	4.7	3.2	3.8	2.3	3.6	7.2	4.4	3.9	1.9	1.2	5.8	2.0	3.7	1.8	6.1

Use the Wilcoxon signed-rank test to investigate the hypothesis that the wear in the two leathers is the same. Use a 5% significance level

7 Trace metals in drinking water affect the flavour of the water and high concentrations can pose a health hazard. The following table shows the zinc concentrations, in milligrams per 1000 litres, of water on the surface and on the river bed at each of 12 locations on a river.

Location	1	2	3	4	5	6	7	8	9	10	11	12
Surface	387	515	721	341	689	599	743	541	717	523	524	445
Bed	435	532	817	366	827	735	812	669	808	622	476	387

Using a Wilcoxon signed-rank test, examine the claim that zinc concentration of water in this river is higher on the river bed than on the surface. Use a 1% significance level

8 A random sample of 11 adults, who had eaten breakfast at 8 am, had their pulse rates measured at 11 am, and then again at 7 pm immediately after they eaten their evening meal. The results were:

Person	A	B	C	D	E	F	G	H	J	K	L
Pulse 11 am	62	75	87	80	89	81	84	82	75	59	68
Pulse 7 pm	60	69	83	79	87	76	75	84	75	58	69

Test whether there is any significant difference, at the 5% level, between pulse rates mid-morning and pulse rates immediately after an evening meal is eaten.

(a) Carry this test out:

(i) using a sign test,

(ii) using a Wilcoxon signed-rank test;

(b) Compare the results from these two non-parametric tests. Why might the Wilcoxon test be preferred to the sign test? [A]

*9 Jim, a market trader, decided to find out whether changing his vegetable supplier would increase his takings. He told a friend, Yasmin, who is a statistician: 'It worked. Yesterday using my old supplier my takings were £180, today with the new supplier my takings were £260.' Yasmin persuaded him to carry out a further trial over a two-week period with the following results.

Day		1st week						2nd week				
	Mon	Tue	Wed	Thu	Fri	Sat	Mon	Tue	Wed	Thu	Fri	Sat
Supplier	Old	Old	New	Old	New	New	New	New	Old	New	Old	Old
Takings (£)	165	199	215	170	387	408	183	204	221	168	345	389

(a) Using the data from the further trial, apply Wilcoxon's signed-rank test, at the 5% significance level, to investigate whether takings increased when the new supplier was used;

(b) Explain why the conclusion drawn from Jim's original 1-day trial may be invalid and the advantages of the trial designed by Yasmin. Include an explanation of experimental error, replication and randomisation in this context. [A]

*10 Eight joints of meat were each cut in half. One half was frozen and wrapped using a standard process and the other half using a new process. The sixteen halves were placed in a freezer and the number of days to spoilage (which can be detected by the colour of the package) was noted for each pack.

Joint number	1	2	3	4	5	6	7	8
Standard process	96	194	149	185	212	237	196	110
New process	117	190	186	776	263	231	242	105

A statistician queried the observation on the new process for joint 4. The experimenter agreed that an error must have been made but said that he was certain that, for this joint, the half frozen by the new process had lasted longer than the other half. He had used the sign test on the eight joints and had accepted, at the 5% significance level, that there was no difference in the median number of days to spoilage.

(a) (i) Confirm, by making any necessary calculations, that the sign test applied to these data does lead to the experimenter's conclusion,

(ii) Use a Wilcoxon's signed-rank test on joints 1, 2, 3, 5, 6, 7 and 8 to test whether there is a difference, at the 5% significance level, in the median number of days to spoilage;

(b) Comment on the validity of using each of the tests on these data. Comment also on the results;

(c) A larger trial is to be carried out and, before the data are collected, you are asked to advise on which test should be used. List advantages of each. [A]

*11 Students on a statistics course are assessed on coursework and by a written examination. The marks obtained by a sample of 14 students were as follows (3 of the students failed to hand in any coursework):

Student	A	B	C	D	E	F	G	H	I	J	K	L	M	N
% Coursework	68	66	0	65	0	66	69	68	70	67	0	67	69	68
% Examination	53	45	67	52	43	71	37	43	68	27	34	79	57	54

(a) Use the sign test, at the 5% significance level on all these results, to examine whether coursework marks are on average higher than examination marks;

(b) Comment on the usefulness or otherwise of these coursework marks as a means of assessing students;

(c) Repeat part **(a)**, excluding the three students who failed to hand in coursework;

(d) Summarise, briefly, your conclusions from the previous three parts. [A]

*12 A university department is deciding which of two research proposals to support. It asked 11 members of staff to read the proposals and to award each of them a mark out of 100. The marks awarded were as follows:

Member of staff	1	2	3	4	5	6	7	8	9	10	11
Proposal 1	89	37	70	21	29	36	11	46	74	47	26
Proposal 2	95	49	69	86	30	99	19	52	30	45	80

(a) Use the sign test at the 5% significance level to test whether proposal 2 is better than proposal 1;

(b) What assumption was it necessary to make in order to carry out the test in part **(a)**?

In view of the erratic nature of the marks awarded, it was decided to ask a further 10 members of staff to award the proposals marks out of 100, but these staff were trained in the features to look for and the method of awarding marks. The new assessment gave the following results:

Member of staff	12	13	14	15	16	17	18	19	20	21
Proposal 1	53	46	60	53	66	59	52	67	63	46
Proposal 2	75	67	69	51	76	59	65	68	72	59

(c) Use a Wilcoxon's signed-rank test, at the 5% significance level, to test whether there is any difference in the average marks awarded to the two proposals by members of staff who had received training;

(d) What assumption is required for part **(c)** that is not required for part **(a)**?

(e) How would the tests have been affected if staff had not been asked to give the proposals a score but had only been asked to say which of the two proposals they thought was better?

[A]

*13 The data shown are the third and fourth round scores of a random sample of five competitors in an open golf tournament.

Competitor	A	B	C	D	E
3rd round	76	75	72	75	79
4th round	70	73	71	68	76

(a) Use Wilcoxon's signed-rank test and a 5% significance level to test whether there is a difference in the median score of all the competitors on the two rounds;

(b) The random variable X follows a binomial distribution with $n = 5$ and $p = 0.5$. Find the probability that $X = 0$;

(c) Explain why your calculation shows that it would be pointless to apply the sign test in part **(a)**;

(d) Find the smallest value of n for which $(0.5)^n < 0.01$;

(e) What is the smallest number of competitors whose scores would be required for there to be any point in applying the sign test with a 1% one-sided significance level;

(f) What assumption is required for Wilcoxon's signed-rank test but is not required for the sign test? [A]

*14 In an investigation into the effects of diet in elderly people a sample of 60 vegetarians over the age of 70 were selected. Each of the selected vegetarians was matched closely as possible for age, gender, general health and exercise habits with a non-vegetarian. The 60 pairs were monitored over a long period of time.

Five years after the start of the investigation both members of eight pairs had died as had one member of a further 23 pairs.

(a) For the eight pairs who had both died the differences in age at death, in months were:

vegetarian − non-vegetarian
    3 38 −27 −2 44 35 3 18

Use Wilcoxon's signed-rank test, at the 1% significance level, to investigate whether there is a difference between the age at death of vegetarians and non-vegetarians;

(b) In 17 of the 23 pairs where one member had died, the surviving member was the vegetarian and in the other six pairs the surviving member was the non-vegetarian. Apply the sign test to the 31 pairs where at least one member had died to investigate, at the 5% significance level, whether there is a difference in age at death of vegetarians and non-vegetarians;

(c) Give one advantage and one disadvantage of the test carried out in part **(a)** compared to the test carried out in part **(b)**;

(d) Discuss, briefly, whether the test shows that eating meat reduces life expectancy. [A]

Key point summary

1 To test the effect of one experimental treatment, a **control group**, which receives no active treatment or the standard treatment, with an **experimental group**, which receives the new treatment, are used.

p82

2 A **placebo** or non-active substance is often given to the **control group** in an experimental trial.

p83

3 **Blind** and **double blind** trials are used to ensure that results are not influenced by expectations, of the subject involved, or the staff looking after the subject, that a new treatment will lead to greater improvement or will cause side effects of a particular type. **Blind** trials are ones where the subject does not know which treatment (placebo/standard or experimental/new) is being used. In **double blind** trials, the staff involved in the trial also do not know which treatment is being given.

p83

4 **Experimental design** is used to eliminate **bias** and reduce **experimental error** in data collection

p84

5 A **paired comparison** is a simple experimental design which can be used to reduce experimental error when two treatments are being compared. In a **paired comparison**, any bias due to differences in the two groups is minimised.

p85

6 The **sign test** and the **Wilcoxon signed-rank test** are **non-parametric tests** which can be used to test for differences between **paired** data.

p89

In the **sign** and the **Wilcoxon tests**, if a pair of readings are identical, that data pair cannot be used in the evaluation of the test statistic. For tied ranks, the average of the relevant values is assigned to each reading.

Test yourself	**What to review**

1 In a trial of a new multi-vitamin and mineral food supplement for children, a group of 150 children are chosen. These children are all the same age, to within three months, and they all scored between 110 and 115 on a recent IQ test.
The children are randomly allocated to receive either the new supplement or a placebo. After six months, they all take another IQ test and the results of the two groups are compared.

Section 5.1

   (a) What is a placebo?

   (b) Which group is the *experimental* group?

   (c) In the context of this question, identify the *control* group and explain why it is needed.

---

2 Jamal decides to carry out a trial to find out whether it is faster to travel to work by bicycle or by bus. Over a four week period, he decides, each day, whether to travel on the bus or by bicycle by tossing a coin.

Section 5.3

At the end of the trial period he has the following results for his twenty journey times (min):

	Mon	**Tue**	**Wed**	**Thur**	**Fri**
Bus	24, 19, 18	12, 16	13, 15, 16	14	15, 18
Bike	21	14, 15	25	10, 17, 14	19, 17

   (a) Explain what is meant by *experimental* error;

   (b) Critically comment on the design of this trial, in particular with reference to any sources of *experimental error*;

   (c) Suggest an improvement to the trial design.

---

3 When a non-parametric sign or Wilcoxon signed-rank test is carried out on a set of paired data and one pair is such that each reading is the same should you:

Section 5.4

   (a) include a difference of 0 and allocate a + sign;

   (b) include a difference of 0 and allocate a − sign;

   (c) ignore the pair completely?

---

4 Under what circumstances can a sign test be carried out on paired data when a Wilcoxon signed-rank test is not possible?

Section 5.5

5

| Test yourself (*continued*) | What to review |

5 To test whether the air temperature at the top of a high tower is lower than the temperature at its base, air temperatures are measured at both top and base at noon on 8 successive days in June. The results (°C) are given below:

Sections 5.4 and 5.5

Day	1	2	3	4	5	6	7	8
Top	22	25	12	23	15	19	20	16
Base	24	29	16	21	18	23	21	20

(a) Use a sign test at the 5% level of significance to test whether the median temperature at the top of the tower is lower than that of the temperature at its base;

(b) Use a Wilcoxon signed-rank test to test the same hypothesis as stated in **(a)** at the same level of significance;

(c) Comment on your results from **(a)** and **(b)** and give a reason why the Wilcoxon signed-rank test might be preferred to the sign test.

| Test yourself | ANSWERS |

1 (a) A non-active treatment which appears identical to the new supplement;

(b) Those taking the new supplement;

(c) Those taking the placebo. Needed so that their results on the second test can be compared with those of the experimental group.

2 (a) Variation due to factors not controlled by Jamal. For example variation in times on Monday by bus is due to experimental error;

(b) Experimental error could be reduced by ensuring he left home at exactly the same time each day and by defining exactly how the timing would be undertaken, etc. Weather conditions would also contribute to experimental error but these are not possible to control;

(c) Travel the same number of times by each day. Tossing a coin or other random process should be used to decide, say, which 2 of the 4 Mondays he should travel by bus.

3 (c).

4 When the sign of each difference is known but it is not possible to rank their magnitudes (or if the population is known not to be symmetrically distributed).

5 (a) $P(1$ or fewer$+) = 0.0352$ significant evidence that median temperature is lower at the top;

(b) $T = 2.5$, cv $= 6$ significant evidence that median temperature is lower at the top;

(c) In this case both tests give the same result. In general, because Wilcoxon's test uses the magnitudes as well as the signs of the differences it is more likely to detect a difference if one exists.

CHAPTER 6

The Mann–Whitney U test – unpaired samples

Learning objectives

After studying this chapter you should be able to:

■ understand the difference between paired and unpaired data
■ carry out a Mann–Whitney U test on data collected as two unpaired samples.

6.1 Mann–Whitney U test

When it is not possible to gather paired data and when you still cannot assume or do not know that the data is normally distributed, a Mann–Whitney U test can be used to test for differences, on average, between the populations from which the two samples are taken. As with other tests, the hypothesis has to be formulated more precisely. In this case it is that the two populations are identical.

> The **Mann–Whitney U test** is a **non-parametric test** which can be used to test for differences between two sets of data which are not **paired**.

For example, a hospital consultant may wish to collect information from the patients in his clinic in order to compare a blood measurement for male and female patients. The data is obviously unpaired and the sample sizes are likely to be different.

Or, perhaps, if Julia, who loves to eat grapefruit every day, believes that the grapefruit in one supermarket are larger than those from another supermarket, she would need to obtain two separate samples: one of grapefruit from Supermarket A and another from Supermarket B. Clearly this is not a paired sample, but two unrelated samples of fruit.

These examples of unpaired samples will be used to explain the procedure for the Mann–Whitney U test. This test, like the Wilcoxon, considers rank values. The ranks are of the actual data, not the differences, as the data is not in pairs.

Sometimes this test is called the Wilcoxon rank-sum test.

Worked example 6.1

A cardiac consultant at a large hospital decides to measure the cholesterol levels of a sample of outpatients seen at her clinic. The resultant readings were:

Females	5.3	2.1	3.8	10.0	1.7	7.1	9.8	1.9	3.1	1.5	
Males	7.3	1.8	4.9	9.2	7.1	4.2	10.2	10.9	3.7	10.5	6.2

In this case, the two samples may well be of different sizes. One is called size m, the other size n.

Test, at the 5% significance level, the hypothesis that there is no difference between male and female cholesterol levels.

Solution

There are two separate samples here: males and females and so an unpaired test is required with:

H$_0$ Average population cholesterol level for females
  = Average population cholesterol level for males
H$_1$ Average population cholesterol level for females
  ≠ Average population cholesterol level for males

Or
H$_0$ two samples come from identical populations
H$_1$ two samples do not come from identical populations: cholesterol levels differ on average.

Two-tailed test significance level 5%.

Ranking the data gives:

The ranking is done with 1 as the lowest.

Females	11	5	8	18	2	13.5	17	4	6	1	
Males	15	3	10	16	13.5	9	19	21	7	20	12

There are two identical readings of 7.1. One is a female, the other a male. The rank order values for these two readings should be 13 and 14. In order to reflect this situation, the **average** of these two rank values is assigned to each of the readings of 7.1. Therefore, the rank 13.5 appears in each list.

For the females, $T_f = 85.5$ and $m = 10$

For the males, $T_m = 145.5$ and $n = 11$

The **test statistic** is labelled **U** where

$$\mathbf{U} = \mathbf{T} - \frac{n(n+1)}{2}$$

T is the sum of the ranks of the sample of size n.

If you have read the note opposite then it is clear that there are *two* possible values for U depending on how the two samples are labelled.

Since it really does not matter which sample is chosen to have size n and which to have size m, you could equally well say:

$$\mathbf{U} = \mathbf{T} - \frac{m(m+1)}{2}$$

T is the sum of the ranks of the sample of size m.

The two possible test statistics are:

$$U = 85.5 - \frac{10(10 + 1)}{2} = \mathbf{30.5} \text{ using female data}$$

or

$$U = 145.5 - \frac{11(11 + 1)}{2} = \mathbf{79.5} \text{ using male data}$$

From the tables, the **lower** critical value for a two-tail test, at a 5% significance level, with samples of size 10 and 11, is **27**.

As the **lower** tail is given, the smaller of the two possible **test statistics** above is the relevant one to use for two-tailed tests.

Thus, with **U** = 30.5, comparing this test statistic to the lower critical value of 27, **U** is **not** less than 27 and therefore **U** does **not** lie in the critical region.

> A check can be made as the two possible test statistics should add up to **mn**. In this case:
>
> $$30.5 + 79.5 = 110$$
> $$mn = (10 \times 11) = 110$$

> **Note.** Alternatively, the upper tail critical value can be evaluated using the formula:
>
> **Upper tail** = *mn* − **lower tail critical**
> = (10 × 11) − 27 = **83**
>
> Then 79.5 is the relevant test statistics and this is **less** than the upper tail and so there is no significant evidence to doubt **H₀**.
>
> Indeed, both 30.5 and 79.5 lie in between the lower and upper tail critical values of 27 and 83 and so, clearly, **H₀** is accepted as true.

6

Conclusion

The test statistic **U** = 30.5 is **greater** than the lower critical value of 27. There is no significant evidence to doubt **H₀** and we conclude that there is no evidence of a difference in average cholesterol levels between males and females in the population.

> **Note.** Theoretically, **H₁** only states that the populations are **not identical**. However, because of the nature of the test, **H₀** is only likely to be rejected if the populations differ on average (whichever measure of average is used).
>
> If the populations had the same mean but very different standard deviations, then **H₀** is **not** likely to be rejected.

Worked example 6.2

Julia has obtained two samples of grapefruit: one from supermarket A and one from supermarket B. These grapefruit were weighed on the same scales and the results obtained for their weights in grams were:

A	164	212	132	140	116	104	167	
B	208	246	197	153	118	169	120	144

Use the Mann–Whitney U test to investigate whether there is any significant evidence, at the 5% level, that the grapefruit from supermarket A are smaller than those from supermarket B.

> The word *smaller* indicates a one-tailed test.

Solution

H_0 Population average weight A = Population average weight B
H_1 Average population difference (weight A − weight B) < 0

One-tailed test significance level 5%.

The first step in carrying out a Mann–Whitney U test is to rank all the data in both samples as though they were all in one group. This is illustrated below.

A	9	14	5	6	2	1	10	
B	13	15	12	8	3	11	4	7

The total for the ranks in each group is then found.

Rank total A, $T_A = 47$,   Rank total B, $T_B = 73$

The two possible values for **U** are:

using sample B, $n = 8$, $T_B = 73$, $U = 73 - \dfrac{8(8+1)}{2} = \mathbf{37}$

or

using sample A, $m = 7$, $T_A = 47$, $U = 47 - \dfrac{7(7+1)}{2} = \mathbf{19}$

The critical values are given in Table 11 for one- or two-tailed tests at 5%.

In this case, for a one-tailed test where we are expecting to find the ranking for A overall **lower** than the ranking for B, the lower value for A of **U = 19** is the relevant test statistic.

The critical value given for $m = 7$, $n = 8$, is 13 for a one-tailed test at 5% and the **test statistic** of 19 is clearly **not lower** than 13.

> **Or**
> H_0 two samples come from identical populations.
> H_1 two samples do not come from identical populations: population A has a lower average weight.

> Again, check that the two possible test statistics add up to *mn*.
> In this case,
> $37 + 19 = 7 \times 8 = 56$.

> If you take a minute to look at Table 11, you will see that the critical values given are symmetrical.
> For $m = 7$ and $n = 8$ the critical value for a one-tailed test is 11 but the critical value is also 11 when $m = 8$ and $n = 7$.

> The **critical region** includes the value quoted in Table 11. A **test statistic** $\leqslant 13$ leads to rejection of H_0.
> The critical values given in the tables are those with significance levels closest to those stated.

Conclusion

The test statistic of 19 is **not less** than the quoted **lower tail critical value** so there is no significant evidence to doubt H_0. We conclude that there is no significant evidence to suggest the population weights differ on average.

6.2 Procedure to follow in order to carry out a Mann–Whitney U test

1 Put **all** data in rank order as though it was in **one** group only.

2 Assign rank 1 to the **smallest** value.

3 Find the **total, T**, of the rank values in each sample.

4 Find the test statistic **U**, where

$$\mathbf{U} = \mathbf{T} - \frac{n(n+1)}{2}$$

There are **two** possible values for **U**, one from each sample.

5 Compare appropriate **U** with relevant critical values from Table 11.

> All the data, in both samples, is **put in rank order** as though it was in one big group. The smallest value is given rank value 1. The total of the rank values in each sample, say, T_A and T_B, are found.

> Two possible values exist for the test statistic, **U**, where:
> $$\mathbf{U} = \mathbf{T} - \frac{n(n+1)}{2}$$
> for T, the total of the rank values in the sample of size n.

Worked example 6.3

A French teacher has decided to try a new approach in getting his students to learn vocabulary. He selects two groups each of six students of similar ability. One group is left to learn their vocabulary in the usual way but the other group is instructed in the new approach.

The two groups are then given a test and the number of words correctly remembered out of the list of 30 is given below:

Usual method	14	17	17	11	16	15
New approach	24	25	29	18	16	19

(a) In the context of this experiment, which group is the control group?

(b) Is the data supplied paired data or unpaired data?

(c) Comment on the experimental design used by this teacher.

(d) Test the hypothesis that the new approach leads to a higher success rate in learning French vocabulary. Use a 5% significance level.

> The use of the word **higher**, indicates a one-tail test.

Solution

(a) The group which is left to learn the vocabulary in the usual way is the control group;

(b) The data is made up of two quite separate groups so it is unpaired data;

> Although the two samples are of the same size, the data is **not** paired.

(c) It would not be possible to test the same person twice, on the same vocabulary list, using both methods, so a paired test is not possible and, as the teacher has ensured the two groups are well matched, hopefully for gender, ability and motivation, the design of this experiment is good;

(d) For number of words in vocabulary list:

H_0 Average correct usual = Average correct new in population

H_1 Average population difference (usual − new) in number correct < 0

One-tailed test significance level 5%.

Ranks are as follows:

Usual method	2	6.5	6.5	1	4.5	3
New approach	10	11	12	8	4.5	9

> There are two occasions with this data when readings are repeated. There are two readings of 16, one in the results from the usual and one from the new method. They share the ranks 4 and 5 and are given an average rank of 4.5 each. Also, there are two readings of 17 in the usual results. These share the rank values 6 and 7 and it doesn't matter which is allocated 6, which 7 or whether they each have rank 6.5 (as given). The total T_u will still be 23.5.

For the usual method, $T_u = 23.5$ and $m = 6$
For the new method, $T_n = 54.5$ and $n = 6$.

The two possible test statistics are:

$$U = 23.5 - \frac{6(6 + 1)}{2} = \textbf{2.5} \text{ using usual results}$$

or

$$U = 54.5 - \frac{6(6 + 1)}{2} = \textbf{33.5} \text{ using new method results}$$

> As you become used to this test, you will not need to find both possible test statistics. For a one-tailed test only one value of U is relevant and for a two-tailed test it will usually be obvious which value will be the smaller.

In this case, for a one-tailed test where we are expecting to find the ranking for the usual method results overall **lower** than the ranking for the results using the new method, the value of for the usual method, $U = 2.5$, is the relevant test statistic to compare with the lower tail critical value.

The critical value given for $m = 6$, $n = 6$, is 7 for a one-tailed test at 5% and the **test statistic** of 2.5 is clearly **lower** than 7.

Conclusion

Since the test statistic 2.5 is much **lower** than the lower tail critical value of 7, there is significant evidence that the two populations differ and students achieve a higher number of correct answers for vocabulary tests using the new approach.

6.3 Comparison of U with critical values

Table 11 gives **lower tail** critical values, therefore, as seen in the previous examples, it is easier, to consider the **lower U** value only.

In **one-tailed tests**, consider which of the two **U** test values is expected to be small and this **lower U** is compared with the **lower, one-tail, critical** value given in Table 11.

In **two-tailed tests**, the **lower U** is compared with the **lower, two-tail, critical** value given in Table 11.

H_0 is rejected if **lower U** $\leqslant$ one-tail **critical value**.

H_0 is rejected if **lower U** $\leqslant$ two-tail **critical value**.

6

> Table 11 tabulates the **lower** tail critical values.

> In **two-tailed** tests, it is only necessary to compare the lower value of U with the **lower tail** critical value from Table 11. If this **lower** test value is greater than the critical value, then both possible U test values will lie between the upper and lower critical values.

> In one-tailed tests H_1, the alternative hypothesis, will determine which value of U should be compared with the lower tail critical value. This will usually, but not always, be the lower value of U.

EXERCISE 6A

1 Twenty students were selected at random from a year group of 121 in a large school. The students were all asked to carry out a visual test and their reaction times(seconds) were noted:

Girls	6.6	7.2	13.1	7.6	4.3	6.7	9.5	3.6	1.4	
Boys	19.7	11.8	7.5	3.0	23.3	6.4	14.1	6.0	15.4	3.8	6.9

Carry out a Mann–Whitney U test at the 5% significance level to test whether girls have faster reaction times than boys for this test.

Comment critically on the design of this experiment.

2 Car batteries are sold as either 'standard' or, for a higher price, as premium 'longer-lasting'. A car hire company decides to test whether the premium batteries do indeed have a longer life. Seven of their small saloon cars are fitted with the standard battery and seven have the premium one fitted.

The length of life (months) of all 14 batteries is given below:

Standard	21	28	37	23	43	40	45
Premium	53	40	48	60	36	51	46

Carry out a Mann–Whitney U test at the 5% significance level to determine whether the premium batteries do last longer. What bias might exist in the way the data was collected for this experiment ?

3 A town fair ran an archery competition for children aged between 12 and 15 years. There were 12 entrants for the competition. Four were girls and eight boys. Their overall scores at the end of the competition were:

Girls	865	975	685	785				
Boys	990	780	955	785	970	985	750	835

At the 5% level of significance, use a suitable non-parametric test to determine whether there is any significant difference between the scores for boys and girls at archery.

4 Applicants for a precision job at a component manufacturer are screened at interview by taking a test to judge their suitability. Two different tests are used randomly for these applicants but the staff recruitment manager is concerned that one test is more difficult than the other.

Results from the 15 most recent tests (marked out of 40) were as follows:

Test 1	23	32	28	29	33	27	30	
Test 2	33	35	37	27	31	28	36	32

Use a Mann–Whitney U test to determine whether there is any evidence, at the 5% significance level, that applicants score lower marks on Test 1.

Explain, with reference to this question, what is meant by *experimental error*.

5 A botanist takes samples of a particular heather from both sides of a hillside. One side faces east and the other side faces west. He measures the length of a random selection of new season plants to examine the hypothesis that plants on the west facing side grow faster than those on the east facing side. The lengths (mm) were found to be as follows:

West	42	29	34	37	35	28	32	28	36
East	38	26	30	27	25	28	31		

Carry out a suitable non-parametric test to test the botanist's hypothesis at the 5% significance level.
Explain your choice of test with reference to the data collected by the botanist. [A]

6 The vitamin content of the flesh of each of a random sample of eight oranges and of a random sample of five lemons was measured. The results are given in milligrams per 10 grams.

Oranges	1.14	1.59	1.57	1.33	1.08	1.27	1.43	1.36
Lemons	1.04	0.95	0.63	1.62	1.11			

Carry out a suitable non-parametric test to investigate at the 5% significance level, whether the average vitamin content of lemons is lower than that of oranges. [A]

7 An economist believes that a typical basket of weekly provisions, purchased by a family of four, costs more in Southville than it does in Nortown. Six stores were randomly selected in each of these two cities and the following costs, for identical baskets of provisions, were observed.

Southville	12.32	13.10	12.11	12.84	12.52	12.71
Nortown	11.95	11.84	12.22	12.67	11.53	12.03

(a) Explain why a paired test would not be appropriate here.

(b) Carry out a Mann–Whitney U test at the 5% significance level to determine whether there is any difference, on average, between the cost of the basket in Southville and Nortown. [A]

*8 The manager of a road haulage firm records the time taken on six occasions for a lorry to travel from the depot to a particular customer's factory. Roadworks are due to start on the usual route so the manager decides to try an alternative route and records the times of eight journeys on this new route.

Time (minutes), old route	34	45	36	48	49	38		
Time (minutes), alternative route	43	35	47	39	58	40	39	51

(a) Use a suitable non-parametric test to investigate, at the 5% significance level, whether there is a difference in the average time taken on the two routes;

(b) One driver had taken 99 minutes on the alternative route. Investigation showed that this was due to losing his way and it was decided to exclude this result from the tests. Comment on this decision.   [A]

*9 A firm is to buy a fleet of cars for use by its representatives and wishes to choose between two alternative models, A and B. It places an advertisement in a local paper offering four free gallons of petrol to anyone who has bought a new car of either model in the last year. The offer is conditional on being willing to answer a questionnaire and to note how far the car goes, under typical driving conditions, on the free petrol supplied. The following data were obtained:

	Miles driven on four gallons of petrol								
Model A	117	136	108	147					
Model B	98	124	96	117	115	126	109	91	108

(a) Use the Mann–Whitney U test to investigate, at the 5% significance level, whether there is a difference between the average petrol consumption of the two models;

(b) List good and bad features of the experimental method and suggest how it could be improved.   [A]

*10 A wholesale fruiterer stocks two varieties of oranges, P and Q, for distribution to retail outlets.
Inspector A measured the weight, x grams, of each of a random sample of 10 oranges of variety P with the following results.

155 146 149 156 161 158 144 148 165 158

A second inspector, B, measured the weight, y grams, of each of a random sample of 11 oranges of variety Q with the following results.

149 146 151 142 153 144 148 152 140 152 137

(a) Indicate a possible source of bias in the collection of these data and suggest how it could have been avoided;

(b) Use a suitable non-parametric test to investigate, at the 5% significance level, the hypothesis that there is no difference between the average weights of the two varieties of oranges. [A]

*11 The manager of a bicycle shop wishes to compare the performance of two makes of tyre. She advertises that anyone buying a tyre of either make during the next week will be given a free inner tube. However they must agree to note the length of time from the new tyre being put on until it sustains a puncture.
The following data were collected.

Make of tyre	Number of days to puncture					
A	43	155	3	167	212	142
	12	96	78	191	77	
B	23	144	34	22		

(a) Use a suitable non-parametric test to investigate, at the 5% significance level, whether the average number of days before sustaining a puncture is the same for the two makes of tyre;

(b) Comment on the method of data collection, the appropriateness of the variable measured, the sample sizes and on any other matters relevant to the experiment;

(c) Explain in the context of this experiment the meaning of Type I and of Type II errors. [A]

*12 The development engineer of a company making razors records the time it takes him to shave, on seven mornings, using a standard razor made by the company. The times, in seconds, were

217   208   254   237   232   243.

(a) Assuming that this may be regarded as a random sample of his shaving times test, at the 1% significance level, the hypothesis that the median time he takes to shave is 3 and a half minutes. Use either the sign test or Wilcoxon's signed-rank test, whichever is more appropriate. Justify your choice of test;

He wishes to compare the time taken by different designs of razor. He decided that rather than test all designs himself it would be quicker to find other employees who would be willing to test one design each. As a preliminary step his assistant agrees to test the standard razor and produces the following times:

> 186   219   168   202   191   184.

(b) Use a Mann–Whitney U test to investigate at the 5% significance level whether the average shaving times of engineer and assistant are the same;

(c) Advise the engineer on how to proceed with his investigation.   [A]

*13 Two analysers are used in a hospital laboratory to measure blood creatinine levels. These are used as a measure of kidney function.

To compare the accuracy of the measurements taken by the two machines a technician took eight specimens of blood and measured their creatinine level (in micromoles per litre) using analyser A. She then measured a further seven samples using analyser B.
The results were as follows:

Analyser A	103	124	130	151	108	96	103	121
Analyser B	142	139	156	164	142	119	117	

(a) Use the Mann–Whitney U test, and a 5% significance level, to investigate for differences between the results of the two analysers.

The technician then realised that, as the analysers had been measuring different samples, whatever the result of the test in part **(a)**, no conclusion about their accuracy could be drawn. She then took eight specimens of blood and measured the creatinine level of each specimen using each machine. The results were as follows:

Specimen 1	1	2	3	4	5	6	7	8
Analyser A	119	173	100	99	77	121	84	73
Analyser B	106	153	83	95	69	123	84	67

(b) Carry out Wilcoxon's signed-rank test, at the 5% level, to compare the performance of the two machines;

(c) Is it now possible to decide which machine is more accurate?
Explain your answer.

A statistician requested that each analyser should be used repeatedly to analyse a standard solution which should give a creatinine level of 90. The results for each machine were as follows:

Analyser A	93	94	96	91	89	93	95	93
Analyser B	98	107	83	85	94	109	89	92

(d) Use Wilcoxon's signed-rank test to test, for each analyser, the hypothesis that the mean measurement is 90. Use a 5% significance level;

(e) What can now be concluded about the performance of the two machines,

(i) from the conclusions reached in part **(d)**,

(ii) from examining (without undertaking further hypothesis testing) the variability of the most recent data? [A]

6

*14 Random samples of apples of two different varieties held in a warehouse were weighed. The weights in grams were as follows:

Variety 1	110.5	89.6	115.0	98.2	113.1	104.3	85.6	92.0		
Variety 2	125.6	118.3	118.0	110.8	116.5	108.7	108.2	104.4	114.4	98.4

(a) Use the Mann–Whitney U test to investigate, at the 5% significance level, whether apples of variety 2 are on average heavier than the apples of variety 1;

(b) Later it transpired that the measuring device used to weigh the apples was faulty and that all the apples were 10 grams heavier than the recorded weight. How would this further information affect your conclusions?

(c) If the recorded weight for variety 1 was correct but variety 2 apples were 10 grams heavier than recorded, state, without further calculation, how your conclusions would be affected. [A]

Key point summary

1 The **Mann–Whitney U test** is a **non-parametric**   *p101*
   test which can be used to test for differences between
   two sets of data which are **not paired**.

2 All the data, in both samples, is **put in rank order**   *p105*
   as though it was in one big group. The smallest value
   is given rank value 1. The total of the rank values in
   each sample, say, T_A and T_B, are found.

3 Two possible values exist for the test statistic, **U**, where: *p105*

$$U = T - \frac{n(n+1)}{2}$$

   for T, the total of the rank values in the sample of size *n*.

4 Table 11 tabulates the **lower** tail critical values.   *p107*

5 In **two-tailed** tests, it is only necessary to compare   *p107*
   the **lower** value of U with the **lower tail** critical value
   from Table 11. If this **lower** test value is greater than
   the critical value, then both possible U test values will
   lie between the upper and lower critical values.

6 In one-tailed tests **H_1**, the alternative hypothesis, will   *p107*
   determine which value of U should be compared with
   the lower tail critical value. This will usually, but not
   always, be the lower value of U.

Test yourself	**What to review**

1 For the following sets of data, say whether the data is paired or unpaired.

Section 6.1

   (a) Height (cm) of two groups of randomly selected males.

Office	146	163	178	154	179	180	142	155
Building site	173	167	182	158	168			

   (b) Pulse rate (beats per min) after 30 mins exercise for a group of 10 visitors to a gym, allocated to either leg exercise or weight training.

Leg exercise	194	186	220	180	130
Weight training	128	197	124	192	148

   (c) Times (seconds) to complete a task for seven people using first their right, then their left hand.

Person	A	B	C	D	E	F	G
Right	29	62	24	17	24	54	83
Left	44	42	29	27	18	76	94

2 Test the hypothesis that the average height of males who work in an office is lower than that of those who work on a building site using the data in **1(a)**.
Use the Mann–Whitney U test at the 5% significance level.

Section 6.2

3 A two-tailed Mann–Whitney U test is carried out on two samples, one of size 8 and the other of size 7. Obtain, using statistical tables, the upper tail and the lower tail critical values if a 5% significance level is used.

Section 6.1

4 For a two-tailed Mann–Whitney U test, using a 5% significance level, determine whether the following test statistics, **U**, where **U** is the lower of the two possible test values, would lead to the rejection of H_0.

Section 6.3

	n	*m*	**U**
(a)	8	12	15
(b)	11	10	49

Test yourself (*continued*)	**What to review**

5 The following data refers to the attitudes of male children from two separate groups.

Section 6.1

Mother working full time	Mother at home full time
23	17
21	18
9	19
30	16
17	14
22	10
19	11
20	

Carry out a Mann–Whitney U test, using a 5% significance level, to determine whether there is a difference on average between attitudes of male children whose mothers work full time and those whose mothers do not work at all.

Test yourself   ANSWERS

1 (a) unpaired;   **(b)** unpaired;   **(c)** paired.

2 H₀ Population average height same for office and building workers
H₁ Population average height higher for building workers. One-tail 5%

O	2	6	10	3	11	12	1	4	$T_O = 49$	$m = 8$
B	9	7	13	5	8				$T_B = 42$	$n = 5$

Possible values $U = 49 - \left(\dfrac{8 \times 9}{2}\right) = 13$ or $U = 42 - \left(\dfrac{5 \times 6}{2}\right) = 27$, cv = 8.

For one-tail test, office workers are expected to be lower. U = 13.
U > 8, so accept **H₀**. Population height is the same.

3 $m = 8$, $n = 7$, two-tail 5%.
Lower tail = 11, upper tail = $(8 \times 7) - 11 = 45$.

4 $m = 12$, $n = 8$, U = 45.
(a) Two-tail 5%, lower cv = 22, U < 22, Reject **H₀**;
(b) $m = 11$, $n = 10$, U = 49.
Two-tail 5%, lower cv = 27, (upper cv = 110 − 31 = 79) U > 27, Accept **H₀**.

5 H₀ Population average attitudes same for mother at home working
H₁ Population average differs. Two-tail 5%

Full-time work	14	12	1	15	13	$9\frac{1}{2}$	11	$6\frac{1}{2}$	$T_F = 82$	$m = 8$
Home	$6\frac{1}{2}$	8	$9\frac{1}{2}$	3	2	4	5		$T_H = 38$	$n = 7$

Possible values $U = 82 - \left(\dfrac{8 \times 7}{2}\right) = 46$ or $U = 38 - \left(\dfrac{8 \times 7}{2}\right) = 10$.
For two-tail test, U = 10, cv = 11.
U < cv. Reject **H₀**. Population average attitudes differ.

S3 Exam style practice paper

Time allowed 1 hour 15 minutes

Answer **all** questions

1 A large smelting plant is situated by a river. Environmental groups are concerned that waste from this plant may be leading to pollution of the river and a series of readings are taken from various accessible sites along the river.

The distance down river from the plant is recorded together with the measure of pH of the water sample taken from this river. A pH value of about 7 is regarded as neutral which is desirable. Readings below 7 indicate acidity and readings above 7 indicate alkalinity. The values obtained are given in the following table:

x Distance (km)	y (pH)
9.4	6.4
6.5	5.0
5.1	4.9
1.6	4.4
2.5	4.6
4.1	4.7
8.6	5.3
10.2	7.4
3.5	4.7
4.5	4.8

(a) Plot a scatter diagram to illustrate the above data and comment on any noticeable features. (*5 marks*)

(b) Calculate the value of Spearman's rank correlation coefficient (*7 marks*)

(c) Stating clearly your null and alternative hypotheses, investigate whether the pH value is associated with the distance. Use a 5% significance level. Interpret your conclusion in the context of the question. (*6 marks*)

(d) The value of the product moment correlation coefficient is 0.880. Explain why you might expect the value of the product correlation coefficient for this data to be substantially different from the value obtained for Spearman's rank correlation coefficient in part **(b)**. *(2 marks)*

2 A random selection of 12 students is made from first year science students at a university in London. These 12 students all take two modules in the second term of their course. After attending these two modules, the students complete an assessment sheet which enables an evaluation of each module to be made.

The two modules have the same level of difficulty and both involve a similar amount of understanding and numerical work.

Module 1 is taught by traditional lecture methods with support offered in smaller groups of around ten students each on three occasions during the 10 week term.

Module 2 is taught using a series of assignments which students complete on their own with weekly tutorial support in a group of five students all term.

The results of the completed evaluations were as follows:

Student	1	2	3	4	5	6	7	8	9	10	11	12
Module 1	45	29	72	52	55	39	85	62	51	35	50	46
Module 2	67	44	75	60	59	34	78	58	64	41	93	57

(a) Explain the advantages of using paired data in testing whether there is any difference between students' assessments of the two modules. *(2 marks)*

(b) Carry out a Wilcoxon signed-rank test using a 5% level of significance to test whether there is any difference between the students' evaluation of the teaching methods for the two modules. *(12 marks)*

(c) At the end of their first year, the students all take five exams and the results of these, together with the results from four pieces of coursework, make up a final first year assessment for each student. From past experience, it is expected that the median mark for this assessment at the end of year 1 will be 70%.

The end of year results for the 12 students involved in this trial were:

    64 60 58 64 59 66 61 50 66 68 72 88

Carry out a sign test at the 5% level of significance to determine whether the first year students have performed below the level expected. *(10 marks)*

(d) How might your results in part **(c)** affect your conclusion in part **(b)**? *(2 marks)*

3 Jeff is given an inexpensive metal detector for his birthday. The detector does not always emit the high-pitched 'bleep' intended to sound when it passes over a metallic object. Also, it can incorrectly emit the 'bleep' when it is passed over non-metallic objects.

Extensive trials have shown that the detector emits the high-pitched 'bleep' correctly when passed over a metallic object with probability 0.9.

It has also been shown that it 'bleeps' incorrectly when passed over a non-metallic object with probability 0.08.

Jeff's mother buried a large number of small objects in the garden. Of these, 45% were metallic and the rest non-metallic.

(a) Find the probability that an object chosen at random from those buried in the garden is non-metallic, but when the detector is passed over it, the 'bleep' is emitted. *(3 marks)*

(b) Find the probability that the detector emits a 'bleep' when passed over an object chosen at random from those buried in the garden. *(3 marks)*

(c) Find the probability that an object is non-metallic given that a 'bleep' was emitted when the detector was passed over it. *(4 marks)*

(d) Find the probability that an object is non-metallic given that **no** 'bleep' was emitted when the detector was passed over it. *(4 marks)*

Time allowed 1 hour 15 minutes

Answer **all** questions

1 The weekly incomes to the nearest £ of 21 people living in a block of flats in a large town are:

143 188 136 165 177 150 138 147 155 168 152
164 144 184 159 161 130 140 165 154 174

At the time that this information was obtained, the median weekly income in the town containing this block of flats was £177.

(a) Use the sign test with a 1% significance level to test whether there is any evidence that the median income of people in the flats differs from £177.　　　(*6 marks*)

(b) How would your conclusions in part (a) be affected in each of the following circumstances,
　　(i) the income of people in the flats is known to follow a negative skew distribution,
　　(ii) the data was obtained from the 21 people who were at home, in the flats, on a Tuesday morning?

Explain your answer in each case.　　　(*5 marks*)

2 Three people, randomly selected from those living in a block of flats in Moss Side were asked to state their monthly household expenditure in pounds. These are given below.

111, 155, 126

A further randomly selected group of people from a block of flats in Chorlton were also asked to state their monthly household expenditure. The results for this group of eleven people are given below.

185, 220, 169, 221, 190, 185, 242, 157, 145, 125, 175

(a) Carry out a Mann–Whitney U test at the 5% significance level to investigate whether there is any difference between the monthly household expenditure of the people in these two blocks of flats.   (*10 marks*)

(b) The purpose of the investigation is to compare the monthly household expenditure of people in Moss Side and Chorlton. Give one good feature and two bad features of the data collection.   (*3 marks*)

3 A questionnaire is given to full time checkout staff in 'Busco' to state whether they consider the maximum number of hours overtime permitted to be too high, about right, or too low.

Excluding staff who have no opinion, the probabilities of answers from a randomly selected members of staff are as follows:

Too high	0.15
About right	0.30
Too low	0.55

(a) What is the probability that if three staff are selected at random:
  (i) all three will answer 'too high',
  (ii) exactly two will answer 'too high',
  (iii) exactly two will give the same answer,
  (iv) exactly two will answer 'too high' given that exactly two give the same answer?   (*11 marks*).

A member of the junior managerial staff at 'Busco' is selected at random from a list of staff at this level working at all the UK 'Busco' stores

B   denotes the event that the junior manager's annual salary is more than £25 000.
C   denotes the event that the junior manager's annual salary is not more than £25 000.
D   denotes the event that the junior manager's annual salary is less than £14 000.
E   denotes the event that the junior manager's annual salary is less than £29 000.

(b) Write down **two** of the events B, C, D and E which are:
  (i) complementary,
  (ii) mutually exclusive but not exhaustive,
  (iii) exhaustive but not mutually exclusive.   (*5 marks*)

4 The following table shows the lengths and widths of a sample of petals from irises of a particular species.

Width (*x* cm)	2.0	1.6	2.6	1.8	2.2	2.8	1.2	0.8	2.4	1.4	1.0
Length (*y* cm)	4.0	3.5	3.8	4.4	4.2	5.0	3.6	2.1	5.4	2.4	2.8

(a) Plot a scatter diagram of length against width. (*3 marks*)

(b) Calculate estimates of:
   (i) the mean and standard deviation of width,
   (ii) the mean and standard deviation of length,
   (iii) the product moment correlation coefficient between length and width. (*7 marks*)

(c) Assuming that the data is a random sample from a bivariate normal distribution with correlation coefficient, ρ, investigate, at the 5% significance level, whether there is evidence of a positive linear relationship between length and width. State clearly your null and alternative hypotheses. (*5 marks*)

The scatter diagram below illustrates the length, y cm, and the width, x cm, of petals from irises of a second species.

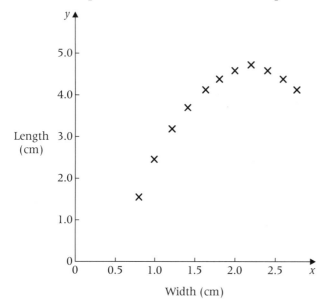

Width (cm)

The following summary statistics relate to the data illustrated in this scatter diagram.

Width: mean 1.8 cm, standard deviation 0.7 cm.
Length: mean 3.8 cm, standard deviation 1.0 cm.

Product moment correlation coefficient of 0.82 between length and width.

(d) Discuss the advisability, or otherwise, of drawing a scatter diagram before undertaking statistical calculations. Relate your discussion to the data on the two species of iris. (*3 marks*)

(e) Comment briefly on the suggestion that the hypothesis $\rho = 0$ should be tested for the second species of iris. (*2 marks*)

Appendix

Table 1 Cumulative binomial distribution function

The tabulated value is $P(X \leqslant x)$, where X has a binomial distribution with parameters n and p.

x	p	0.01	0.02	0.03	0.04	0.05	0.06	0.07	0.08	0.09	0.10	0.15	0.20	0.25	0.30	0.35	0.40	0.45	0.50	p	x
$n = 2$	0	0.9801	0.9604	0.9409	0.9216	0.9025	0.8836	0.8649	0.8464	0.8281	0.8100	0.7225	0.6400	0.5625	0.4900	0.4225	0.3600	0.3025	0.2500		0
	1	0.9999	0.9996	0.9991	0.9984	0.9975	0.9964	0.9951	0.9936	0.9919	0.9900	0.9775	0.9600	0.9375	0.9100	0.8775	0.8400	0.7975	0.7500		1
	2	1.0000	1.0000	1.0000	1.0000	1.0000	1.0000	1.0000	1.0000	1.0000	1.0000	1.0000	1.0000	1.0000	1.0000	1.0000	1.0000	1.0000	1.0000		2
$n = 3$	0	0.9703	0.9412	0.9127	0.8847	0.8574	0.8306	0.8044	0.7787	0.7536	0.7290	0.6141	0.5120	0.4219	0.3430	0.2746	0.2160	0.1664	0.1250		0
	1	0.9997	0.9988	0.9974	0.9953	0.9928	0.9896	0.9860	0.9818	0.9772	0.9720	0.9393	0.8960	0.8438	0.7840	0.7183	0.6480	0.5748	0.5000		1
	2	1.0000	1.0000	1.0000	0.9999	0.9999	0.9998	0.9997	0.9995	0.9993	0.9990	0.9966	0.9920	0.9844	0.9730	0.9571	0.9360	0.9089	0.8750		2
	3				1.0000	1.0000	1.0000	1.0000	1.0000	1.0000	1.0000	1.0000	1.0000	1.0000	1.0000	1.0000	1.0000	1.0000	1.0000		3
$n = 4$	0	0.9606	0.9224	0.8853	0.8493	0.8145	0.7807	0.7481	0.7164	0.6857	0.6561	0.5220	0.4096	0.3164	0.2401	0.1785	0.1296	0.0915	0.0625		0
	1	0.9994	0.9977	0.9948	0.9909	0.9860	0.9801	0.9733	0.9656	0.9570	0.9477	0.8905	0.8192	0.7383	0.6517	0.5630	0.4752	0.3910	0.3125		1
	2	1.0000	1.0000	0.9999	0.9998	0.9995	0.9992	0.9987	0.9981	0.9973	0.9963	0.9880	0.9728	0.9492	0.9163	0.8735	0.8208	0.7585	0.6875		2
	3			1.0000	1.0000	1.0000	1.0000	1.0000	1.0000	0.9999	0.9999	0.9995	0.9984	0.9961	0.9919	0.9850	0.9744	0.9590	0.9375		3
	4									1.0000	1.0000	1.0000	1.0000	1.0000	1.0000	1.0000	1.0000	1.0000	1.0000		4
$n = 5$	0	0.9510	0.9039	0.8587	0.8154	0.7738	0.7339	0.6957	0.6591	0.6240	0.5905	0.4437	0.3277	0.2373	0.1681	0.1160	0.0778	0.0503	0.0313		0
	1	0.9990	0.9962	0.9915	0.9852	0.9774	0.9681	0.9575	0.9456	0.9326	0.9185	0.8352	0.7373	0.6328	0.5282	0.4284	0.3370	0.2562	0.1875		1
	2	1.0000	0.9999	0.9997	0.9994	0.9988	0.9980	0.9969	0.9955	0.9937	0.9914	0.9734	0.9421	0.8965	0.8369	0.7648	0.6826	0.5931	0.5000		2
	3		1.0000	1.0000	1.0000	1.0000	0.9999	0.9999	0.9998	0.9997	0.9995	0.9978	0.9933	0.9844	0.9692	0.9460	0.9130	0.8688	0.8125		3
	4					1.0000	1.0000	1.0000	1.0000	1.0000	1.0000	0.9999	0.9997	0.9990	0.9976	0.9947	0.9898	0.9815	0.9688		4
	5										1.0000	1.0000	1.0000	1.0000	1.0000	1.0000	1.0000	1.0000	1.0000		5
$n = 6$	0	0.9415	0.8858	0.8330	0.7828	0.7351	0.6899	0.6470	0.6064	0.5679	0.5314	0.3771	0.2621	0.1780	0.1176	0.0754	0.0467	0.0277	0.0156		0
	1	0.9985	0.9943	0.9875	0.9784	0.9672	0.9541	0.9392	0.9227	0.9048	0.8857	0.7765	0.6554	0.5339	0.4202	0.3191	0.2333	0.1636	0.1094		1
	2	1.0000	0.9998	0.9995	0.9988	0.9978	0.9962	0.9942	0.9915	0.9882	0.9842	0.9527	0.9011	0.8306	0.7443	0.6471	0.5443	0.4415	0.3438		2
	3		1.0000	1.0000	1.0000	0.9999	0.9998	0.9997	0.9995	0.9992	0.9987	0.9941	0.9830	0.9624	0.9295	0.8826	0.8208	0.7447	0.6563		3
	4					1.0000	1.0000	1.0000	1.0000	1.0000	0.9999	0.9996	0.9984	0.9954	0.9891	0.9777	0.9590	0.9308	0.8906		4
	5									1.0000	1.0000	0.9999	0.9998	0.9993	0.9982	0.9959	0.9917	0.9844		5
	6											1.0000	1.0000	1.0000	1.0000	1.0000	1.0000	1.0000	1.0000		6
$n = 7$	0	0.9321	0.8681	0.8080	0.7514	0.6983	0.6485	0.6017	0.5578	0.5168	0.4783	0.3206	0.2097	0.1335	0.0824	0.0490	0.0280	0.0152	0.0078		0
	1	0.9980	0.9921	0.9829	0.9706	0.9556	0.9382	0.9187	0.8974	0.8745	0.8503	0.7166	0.5767	0.4449	0.3294	0.2338	0.1586	0.1024	0.0625		1
	2	1.0000	0.9997	0.9991	0.9980	0.9962	0.9937	0.9903	0.9860	0.9807	0.9743	0.9262	0.8520	0.7564	0.6471	0.5323	0.4199	0.3164	0.2266		2
	3		1.0000	1.0000	0.9999	0.9998	0.9996	0.9993	0.9988	0.9982	0.9973	0.9879	0.9667	0.9294	0.8740	0.8002	0.7102	0.6083	0.5000		3
	4				1.0000	1.0000	1.0000	1.0000	0.9999	0.9999	0.9998	0.9988	0.9953	0.9871	0.9712	0.9444	0.9037	0.8471	0.7734		4
	5								1.0000	1.0000	1.0000	0.9999	0.9996	0.9987	0.9962	0.9910	0.9812	0.9643	0.9375		5
	6											1.0000	1.0000	0.9999	0.9998	0.9994	0.9984	0.9963	0.9922		6
	7													1.0000	1.0000	1.0000	1.0000	1.0000	1.0000		7
$n = 8$	0	0.9227	0.8508	0.7837	0.7214	0.6634	0.6096	0.5596	0.5132	0.4703	0.4305	0.2725	0.1678	0.1001	0.0576	0.0319	0.0168	0.0084	0.0039		0
	1	0.9973	0.9897	0.9777	0.9619	0.9428	0.9208	0.8965	0.8702	0.8423	0.8131	0.6572	0.5033	0.3671	0.2553	0.1691	0.1064	0.0632	0.0352		1
	2	0.9999	0.9996	0.9987	0.9969	0.9942	0.9904	0.9853	0.9789	0.9711	0.9619	0.8948	0.7969	0.6785	0.5518	0.4278	0.3154	0.2201	0.1445		2
	3	1.0000	1.0000	0.9999	0.9998	0.9996	0.9993	0.9987	0.9978	0.9966	0.9950	0.9786	0.9437	0.8862	0.8059	0.7064	0.5941	0.4770	0.3633		3
	4			1.0000	1.0000	1.0000	1.0000	0.9999	0.9999	0.9997	0.9996	0.9971	0.9896	0.9727	0.9420	0.8939	0.8263	0.7396	0.6367		4
	5							1.0000	1.0000	1.0000	1.0000	0.9998	0.9988	0.9958	0.9887	0.9747	0.9502	0.9115	0.8555		5
	6											1.0000	0.9999	0.9996	0.9987	0.9964	0.9915	0.9819	0.9648		6
	7												1.0000	1.0000	0.9999	0.9998	0.9993	0.9983	0.9961		7
	8														1.0000	1.0000	1.0000	1.0000	1.0000		8

Table 1 Cumulative binomial distribution function (cont.)

x	0.01	0.02	0.03	0.04	0.05	0.06	0.07	0.08	0.09	0.10	0.15	0.20	0.25	0.30	0.35	0.40	0.45	0.50	x
n = 9 0	0.9135	0.8337	0.7602	0.6925	0.6302	0.5730	0.5204	0.4722	0.4279	0.3874	0.2316	0.1342	0.0751	0.0404	0.0207	0.0101	0.0046	0.0020	0
1	0.9966	0.9869	0.9718	0.9522	0.9288	0.9022	0.8729	0.8417	0.8088	0.7748	0.5995	0.4362	0.3003	0.1960	0.1211	0.0705	0.0385	0.0195	1
2	0.9999	0.9994	0.9980	0.9955	0.9916	0.9862	0.9791	0.9702	0.9595	0.9470	0.8591	0.7382	0.6007	0.4628	0.3373	0.2318	0.1495	0.0898	2
3	1.0000	1.0000	0.9999	0.9997	0.9994	0.9987	0.9977	0.9963	0.9943	0.9917	0.9661	0.9144	0.8343	0.7297	0.6089	0.4826	0.3614	0.2539	3
4			1.0000	1.0000	1.0000	0.9999	0.9998	0.9997	0.9995	0.9991	0.9944	0.9804	0.9511	0.9012	0.8283	0.7334	0.6214	0.5000	4
5						1.0000	1.0000	1.0000	1.0000	0.9999	0.9994	0.9969	0.9900	0.9747	0.9464	0.9006	0.8342	0.7461	5
6										1.0000	1.0000	0.9997	0.9987	0.9957	0.9888	0.9750	0.9502	0.9102	6
7												1.0000	0.9999	0.9996	0.9986	0.9962	0.9909	0.9805	7
8													1.0000	1.0000	0.9999	0.9997	0.9992	0.9980	8
9															1.0000	1.0000	1.0000	1.0000	9
n = 10 0	0.9044	0.8171	0.7374	0.6648	0.5987	0.5386	0.4840	0.4344	0.3894	0.3487	0.1969	0.1074	0.0563	0.0282	0.0135	0.0060	0.0025	0.0010	0
1	0.9957	0.9838	0.9655	0.9418	0.9139	0.8824	0.8483	0.8121	0.7746	0.7361	0.5443	0.3758	0.2440	0.1493	0.0860	0.0464	0.0233	0.0107	1
2	0.9999	0.9991	0.9972	0.9938	0.9885	0.9812	0.9717	0.9599	0.9460	0.9298	0.8202	0.6778	0.5256	0.3828	0.2616	0.1673	0.0996	0.0547	2
3	1.0000	1.0000	0.9999	0.9996	0.9990	0.9980	0.9964	0.9942	0.9912	0.9872	0.9500	0.8791	0.7759	0.6496	0.5138	0.3823	0.2660	0.1719	3
4			1.0000	1.0000	0.9999	0.9998	0.9997	0.9994	0.9990	0.9984	0.9901	0.9672	0.9219	0.8497	0.7515	0.6331	0.5044	0.3770	4
5					1.0000	1.0000	1.0000	1.0000	0.9999	0.9999	0.9986	0.9936	0.9803	0.9527	0.9051	0.8338	0.7384	0.6230	5
6									1.0000	1.0000	0.9999	0.9991	0.9965	0.9894	0.9740	0.9452	0.8980	0.8281	6
7											1.0000	0.9999	0.9996	0.9984	0.9952	0.9877	0.9726	0.9453	7
8												1.0000	1.0000	0.9999	0.9995	0.9983	0.9955	0.9893	8
9														1.0000	1.0000	0.9999	0.9997	0.9990	9
10																1.0000	1.0000	1.0000	10
n = 11 0	0.8953	0.8007	0.7153	0.6382	0.5688	0.5063	0.4501	0.3996	0.3544	0.3138	0.1673	0.0859	0.0422	0.0198	0.0088	0.0036	0.0014	0.0005	0
1	0.9948	0.9805	0.9587	0.9308	0.8981	0.8618	0.8228	0.7819	0.7399	0.6974	0.4922	0.3221	0.1971	0.1130	0.0606	0.0302	0.0139	0.0059	1
2	0.9998	0.9988	0.9963	0.9917	0.9848	0.9752	0.9630	0.9481	0.9305	0.9104	0.7788	0.6174	0.4552	0.3127	0.2001	0.1189	0.0652	0.0327	2
3	1.0000	1.0000	0.9998	0.9993	0.9984	0.9970	0.9947	0.9915	0.9871	0.9815	0.9306	0.8389	0.7133	0.5696	0.4256	0.2963	0.1911	0.1133	3
4			1.0000	1.0000	0.9999	0.9997	0.9995	0.9990	0.9983	0.9972	0.9841	0.9496	0.8854	0.7897	0.6683	0.5328	0.3971	0.2744	4
5					1.0000	1.0000	1.0000	0.9999	0.9998	0.9997	0.9973	0.9883	0.9657	0.9218	0.8513	0.7535	0.6331	0.5000	5
6								1.0000	1.0000	1.0000	0.9997	0.9980	0.9924	0.9784	0.9499	0.9006	0.8262	0.7256	6
7											1.0000	0.9998	0.9988	0.9957	0.9878	0.9707	0.9390	0.8867	7
8												1.0000	0.9999	0.9994	0.9980	0.9941	0.9852	0.9673	8
9													1.0000	1.0000	0.9998	0.9993	0.9978	0.9941	9
10															1.0000	1.0000	0.9998	0.9995	10
11																		1.0000	11
n = 12 0	0.8864	0.7847	0.6938	0.6127	0.5404	0.4759	0.4186	0.3677	0.3225	0.2824	0.1422	0.0687	0.0317	0.0138	0.0057	0.0022	0.0008	0.0002	0
1	0.9938	0.9769	0.9514	0.9191	0.8816	0.8405	0.7967	0.7513	0.7052	0.6590	0.4435	0.2749	0.1584	0.0850	0.0424	0.0196	0.0083	0.0032	1
2	0.9998	0.9985	0.9952	0.9893	0.9804	0.9684	0.9532	0.9348	0.9134	0.8891	0.7358	0.5583	0.3907	0.2528	0.1513	0.0834	0.0421	0.0193	2
3	1.0000	0.9999	0.9997	0.9990	0.9978	0.9957	0.9925	0.9880	0.9820	0.9744	0.9078	0.7946	0.6488	0.4925	0.3467	0.2253	0.1345	0.0730	3
4		1.0000	1.0000	0.9999	0.9998	0.9996	0.9991	0.9984	0.9973	0.9957	0.9761	0.9274	0.8424	0.7237	0.5833	0.4382	0.3044	0.1938	4
5				1.0000	1.0000	1.0000	0.9999	0.9998	0.9997	0.9995	0.9954	0.9806	0.9456	0.8822	0.7873	0.6652	0.5269	0.3872	5
6							1.0000	1.0000	1.0000	0.9999	0.9993	0.9961	0.9857	0.9614	0.9154	0.8418	0.7393	0.6128	6
7										1.0000	0.9999	0.9994	0.9972	0.9905	0.9745	0.9427	0.8883	0.8062	7
8											1.0000	0.9999	0.9996	0.9983	0.9944	0.9847	0.9644	0.9270	8
9												1.0000	1.0000	0.9998	0.9992	0.9972	0.9921	0.9807	9
10														1.0000	0.9999	0.9997	0.9989	0.9968	10
11															1.0000	1.0000	0.9999	0.9998	11
12																	1.0000	1.0000	12
n = 13 0	0.8775	0.7690	0.6730	0.5882	0.5133	0.4474	0.3893	0.3383	0.2935	0.2542	0.1209	0.0550	0.0238	0.0097	0.0037	0.0013	0.0004	0.0001	0
1	0.9928	0.9730	0.9436	0.9068	0.8646	0.8186	0.7702	0.7206	0.6707	0.6213	0.3983	0.2336	0.1267	0.0637	0.0296	0.0126	0.0049	0.0017	1
2	0.9997	0.9980	0.9938	0.9865	0.9755	0.9608	0.9422	0.9201	0.8946	0.8661	0.6920	0.5017	0.3326	0.2025	0.1132	0.0579	0.0269	0.0112	2
3	1.0000	0.9999	0.9995	0.9986	0.9969	0.9940	0.9897	0.9837	0.9758	0.9658	0.8820	0.7473	0.5843	0.4206	0.2783	0.1686	0.0929	0.0461	3
4		1.0000	1.0000	0.9999	0.9997	0.9993	0.9987	0.9976	0.9959	0.9935	0.9658	0.9009	0.7940	0.6543	0.5005	0.3530	0.2279	0.1334	4
5				1.0000	1.0000	0.9999	0.9999	0.9997	0.9995	0.9991	0.9925	0.9700	0.9198	0.8346	0.7159	0.5744	0.4268	0.2905	5
6						1.0000	1.0000	1.0000	0.9999	0.9999	0.9987	0.9930	0.9757	0.9376	0.8705	0.7712	0.6437	0.5000	6
7									1.0000	1.0000	0.9998	0.9988	0.9944	0.9818	0.9538	0.9023	0.8212	0.7095	7
8											1.0000	0.9998	0.9990	0.9960	0.9874	0.9679	0.9302	0.8666	8
9												1.0000	0.9999	0.9993	0.9975	0.9922	0.9797	0.9539	9
10													1.0000	0.9999	0.9997	0.9987	0.9959	0.9888	10
11														1.0000	1.0000	0.9999	0.9995	0.9983	11
12																1.0000	1.0000	0.9999	12
13																		1.0000	13

Table I Cumulative binomial distribution function (cont.)

x	0.01	0.02	0.03	0.04	0.05	0.06	0.07	0.08	0.09	0.10	0.15	0.20	0.25	0.30	0.35	0.40	0.45	0.50	x
n = 14 0	0.8687	0.7536	0.6528	0.5647	0.4877	0.4205	0.3620	0.3112	0.2670	0.2288	0.1028	0.0440	0.0178	0.0068	0.0024	0.0008	0.0002	0.0001	0
1	0.9916	0.9690	0.9355	0.8941	0.8470	0.7963	0.7436	0.6900	0.6368	0.5846	0.3567	0.1979	0.1010	0.0475	0.0205	0.0081	0.0029	0.0009	1
2	0.9997	0.9975	0.9923	0.9833	0.9699	0.9522	0.9302	0.9042	0.8745	0.8416	0.6479	0.4481	0.2811	0.1608	0.0839	0.0398	0.0170	0.0065	2
3	1.0000	0.9999	0.9994	0.9981	0.9958	0.9920	0.9864	0.9786	0.9685	0.9559	0.8535	0.6982	0.5213	0.3552	0.2205	0.1243	0.0632	0.0287	3
4		1.0000	1.0000	0.9998	0.9996	0.9990	0.9980	0.9965	0.9941	0.9908	0.9533	0.8702	0.7415	0.5842	0.4227	0.2793	0.1672	0.0898	4
5				1.0000	1.0000	0.9999	0.9998	0.9996	0.9992	0.9985	0.9885	0.9561	0.8883	0.7805	0.6405	0.4859	0.3373	0.2120	5
6						1.0000	1.0000	1.0000	0.9999	0.9998	0.9978	0.9884	0.9617	0.9067	0.8164	0.6925	0.5461	0.3953	6
7									1.0000	1.0000	0.9997	0.9976	0.9897	0.9685	0.9247	0.8499	0.7414	0.6047	7
8											1.0000	0.9996	0.9978	0.9917	0.9757	0.9417	0.8811	0.7880	8
9												1.0000	0.9997	0.9983	0.9940	0.9825	0.9574	0.9102	9
10													1.0000	0.9998	0.9989	0.9961	0.9886	0.9713	10
11														1.0000	0.9999	0.9994	0.9978	0.9935	11
12															1.0000	0.9999	0.9997	0.9991	12
13																1.0000	1.0000	0.9999	13
14																		1.0000	14
n = 15 0	0.8601	0.7386	0.6333	0.5421	0.4633	0.3953	0.3367	0.2863	0.2430	0.2059	0.0874	0.0352	0.0134	0.0047	0.0016	0.0005	0.0001	0.0000	0
1	0.9904	0.9647	0.9270	0.8809	0.8290	0.7738	0.7168	0.6597	0.6035	0.5490	0.3186	0.1671	0.0802	0.0353	0.0142	0.0052	0.0017	0.0005	1
2	0.9996	0.9970	0.9906	0.9797	0.9638	0.9429	0.9171	0.8870	0.8531	0.8159	0.6042	0.3980	0.2361	0.1268	0.0617	0.0271	0.0107	0.0037	2
3	1.0000	0.9998	0.9992	0.9976	0.9945	0.9896	0.9825	0.9727	0.9601	0.9444	0.8227	0.6482	0.4613	0.2969	0.1727	0.0905	0.0424	0.0176	3
4		1.0000	0.9999	0.9998	0.9994	0.9986	0.9972	0.9950	0.9918	0.9873	0.9383	0.8358	0.6865	0.5155	0.3519	0.2173	0.1204	0.0592	4
5			1.0000	1.0000	0.9999	0.9999	0.9997	0.9993	0.9987	0.9978	0.9832	0.9389	0.8516	0.7216	0.5643	0.4032	0.2608	0.1509	5
6						1.0000	1.0000	0.9999	0.9998	0.9997	0.9964	0.9819	0.9434	0.8689	0.7548	0.6098	0.4522	0.3036	6
7								1.0000	1.0000	1.0000	0.9994	0.9958	0.9827	0.9500	0.8868	0.7869	0.6535	0.5000	7
8											0.9999	0.9992	0.9958	0.9848	0.9578	0.9050	0.8182	0.6964	8
9											1.0000	0.9999	0.9992	0.9963	0.9876	0.9662	0.9231	0.8491	9
10												1.0000	0.9999	0.9993	0.9972	0.9907	0.9745	0.9408	10
11													1.0000	0.9999	0.9995	0.9981	0.9937	0.9824	11
12														1.0000	0.9999	0.9997	0.9989	0.9963	12
13															1.0000	1.0000	0.9999	0.9995	13
14																	1.0000	1.0000	14
n = 20 0	0.8179	0.6676	0.5438	0.4420	0.3585	0.2901	0.2342	0.1887	0.1516	0.1216	0.0388	0.0115	0.0032	0.0008	0.0002	0.0000	0.0000	0.0000	0
1	0.9831	0.9401	0.8802	0.8103	0.7358	0.6605	0.5869	0.5169	0.4516	0.3917	0.1756	0.0692	0.0243	0.0076	0.0021	0.0005	0.0001	0.0000	1
2	0.9990	0.9929	0.9790	0.9561	0.9245	0.8850	0.8390	0.7879	0.7334	0.6769	0.4049	0.2061	0.0913	0.0355	0.0121	0.0036	0.0009	0.0002	2
3	1.0000	0.9994	0.9973	0.9926	0.9841	0.9710	0.9529	0.9294	0.9007	0.8670	0.6477	0.4114	0.2252	0.1071	0.0444	0.0160	0.0049	0.0013	3
4		1.0000	0.9997	0.9990	0.9974	0.9944	0.9893	0.9817	0.9710	0.9568	0.8298	0.6296	0.4148	0.2375	0.1182	0.0510	0.0189	0.0059	4
5			1.0000	0.9999	0.9997	0.9991	0.9981	0.9962	0.9932	0.9887	0.9327	0.8042	0.6172	0.4164	0.2454	0.1256	0.0553	0.0207	5
6				1.0000	1.0000	0.9999	0.9997	0.9994	0.9987	0.9976	0.9781	0.9133	0.7858	0.6080	0.4166	0.2500	0.1299	0.0577	6
7						1.0000	1.0000	0.9999	0.9998	0.9996	0.9941	0.9679	0.8982	0.7723	0.6010	0.4159	0.2520	0.1316	7
8								1.0000	1.0000	0.9999	0.9987	0.9900	0.9591	0.8867	0.7624	0.5956	0.4143	0.2517	8
9										1.0000	0.9998	0.9974	0.9861	0.9520	0.8782	0.7553	0.5914	0.4119	9
10											1.0000	0.9994	0.9961	0.9829	0.9468	0.8725	0.7507	0.5881	10
11												0.9999	0.9991	0.9949	0.9804	0.9435	0.8692	0.7483	11
12												1.0000	0.9998	0.9987	0.9940	0.9790	0.9420	0.8684	12
13													1.0000	0.9997	0.9985	0.9935	0.9786	0.9423	13
14														1.0000	0.9997	0.9984	0.9936	0.9793	14
15															1.0000	0.9997	0.9985	0.9941	15
16																1.0000	0.9997	0.9987	16
17																	1.0000	0.9998	17
18																		1.0000	18
n = 25 0	0.7778	0.6035	0.4670	0.3604	0.2774	0.2129	0.1630	0.1244	0.0946	0.0718	0.0172	0.0038	0.0008	0.0001	0.0000	0.0000	0.0000	0.0000	0
1	0.9742	0.9114	0.8280	0.7358	0.6424	0.5527	0.4696	0.3947	0.3286	0.2712	0.0931	0.0274	0.0070	0.0016	0.0003	0.0001	0.0000	0.0000	1
2	0.9980	0.9868	0.9620	0.9235	0.8729	0.8129	0.7466	0.6768	0.6063	0.5371	0.2537	0.0982	0.0321	0.0090	0.0021	0.0004	0.0001	0.0000	2
3	0.9999	0.9986	0.9938	0.9835	0.9659	0.9402	0.9064	0.8649	0.8169	0.7636	0.4711	0.2340	0.0962	0.0332	0.0097	0.0024	0.0005	0.0001	3
4	1.0000	0.9999	0.9992	0.9972	0.9928	0.9850	0.9726	0.9549	0.9314	0.9020	0.6821	0.4207	0.2137	0.0905	0.0320	0.0095	0.0023	0.0005	4
5		1.0000	0.9999	0.9996	0.9988	0.9969	0.9935	0.9877	0.9790	0.9666	0.8385	0.6167	0.3783	0.1935	0.0826	0.0294	0.0086	0.0020	5
6			1.0000	1.0000	0.9998	0.9995	0.9987	0.9972	0.9946	0.9905	0.9305	0.7800	0.5611	0.3407	0.1734	0.0736	0.0258	0.0073	6
7					1.0000	0.9999	0.9998	0.9995	0.9989	0.9977	0.9745	0.8909	0.7265	0.5118	0.3061	0.1536	0.0639	0.0216	7
8						1.0000	1.0000	0.9999	0.9998	0.9995	0.9920	0.9532	0.8506	0.6769	0.4668	0.2735	0.1340	0.0539	8
9								1.0000	1.0000	0.9999	0.9979	0.9827	0.9287	0.8106	0.6303	0.4246	0.2424	0.1148	9
10										1.0000	0.9995	0.9944	0.9703	0.9022	0.7712	0.5858	0.3843	0.2122	10
11											0.9999	0.9985	0.9893	0.9558	0.8746	0.7323	0.5426	0.3450	11
12											1.0000	0.9996	0.9966	0.9825	0.9396	0.8462	0.6937	0.5000	12
13												0.9999	0.9991	0.9940	0.9745	0.9222	0.8173	0.6550	13
14												1.0000	0.9998	0.9982	0.9907	0.9656	0.9040	0.7878	14
15													1.0000	0.9995	0.9971	0.9868	0.9560	0.8852	15
16														0.9999	0.9992	0.9957	0.9826	0.9461	16
17														1.0000	0.9998	0.9988	0.9942	0.9784	17
18															1.0000	0.9997	0.9984	0.9927	18
19																0.9999	0.9996	0.9980	19
20																1.0000	0.9999	0.9995	20
21																	1.0000	0.9999	21
22																		1.0000	22

Table 1 Cumulative binomial distribution function (cont.)

n = 30

x	0.01	0.02	0.03	0.04	0.05	0.06	0.07	0.08	0.09	0.10	0.15	0.20	0.25	0.30	0.35	0.40	0.45	0.50	x
0	0.7397	0.5455	0.4010	0.2939	0.2146	0.1563	0.1134	0.0820	0.0591	0.0424	0.0076	0.0012	0.0002	0.0000	0.0000	0.0000	0.0000	0.0000	0
1	0.9639	0.8795	0.7731	0.6612	0.5535	0.4555	0.3694	0.2958	0.2343	0.1837	0.0480	0.0105	0.0020	0.0003	0.0000	0.0000	0.0000	0.0000	1
2	0.9967	0.9783	0.9399	0.8831	0.8122	0.7324	0.6487	0.5654	0.4855	0.4114	0.1514	0.0442	0.0106	0.0021	0.0003	0.0000	0.0000	0.0000	2
3	0.9998	0.9971	0.9881	0.9694	0.9392	0.8974	0.8450	0.7842	0.7175	0.6474	0.3217	0.1227	0.0374	0.0093	0.0019	0.0003	0.0000	0.0000	3
4	1.0000	0.9997	0.9982	0.9937	0.9844	0.9685	0.9447	0.9126	0.8723	0.8245	0.5245	0.2552	0.0979	0.0302	0.0075	0.0015	0.0002	0.0000	4
5		1.0000	0.9998	0.9989	0.9967	0.9921	0.9838	0.9707	0.9519	0.9268	0.7106	0.4275	0.2026	0.0766	0.0233	0.0057	0.0011	0.0002	5
6			1.0000	0.9999	0.9994	0.9983	0.9960	0.9918	0.9848	0.9742	0.8474	0.6070	0.3481	0.1595	0.0586	0.0172	0.0040	0.0007	6
7				1.0000	0.9999	0.9997	0.9992	0.9980	0.9959	0.9922	0.9302	0.7608	0.5143	0.2814	0.1238	0.0435	0.0121	0.0026	7
8					1.0000	1.0000	0.9999	0.9996	0.9990	0.9980	0.9722	0.8713	0.6736	0.4315	0.2247	0.0940	0.0312	0.0081	8
9						1.0000	0.9999	0.9998	0.9995	0.9993	0.9903	0.9389	0.8034	0.5888	0.3575	0.1763	0.0694	0.0214	9
10								1.0000	1.0000	0.9999	0.9971	0.9744	0.8943	0.7304	0.5078	0.2915	0.1350	0.0494	10
11										1.0000	0.9992	0.9905	0.9493	0.8407	0.6548	0.4311	0.2327	0.1002	11
12											0.9998	0.9969	0.9784	0.9155	0.7802	0.5785	0.3592	0.1808	12
13											1.0000	0.9991	0.9918	0.9599	0.8737	0.7145	0.5025	0.2923	13
14												0.9998	0.9973	0.9831	0.9348	0.8246	0.6448	0.4278	14
15												0.9999	0.9992	0.9936	0.9699	0.9029	0.7691	0.5722	15
16												1.0000	0.9998	0.9979	0.9876	0.9519	0.8644	0.7077	16
17													0.9999	0.9994	0.9955	0.9788	0.9286	0.8192	17
18													1.0000	0.9998	0.9986	0.9917	0.9666	0.8998	18
19														1.0000	0.9996	0.9971	0.9862	0.9506	19
20															0.9999	0.9991	0.9950	0.9786	20
21															1.0000	0.9998	0.9984	0.9919	21
22																1.0000	0.9996	0.9974	22
23																	0.9999	0.9993	23
24																	1.0000	0.9998	24
25																		1.0000	25

n = 40

x	0.01	0.02	0.03	0.04	0.05	0.06	0.07	0.08	0.09	0.10	0.15	0.20	0.25	0.30	0.35	0.40	0.45	0.50	x
0	0.6690	0.4457	0.2957	0.1954	0.1285	0.0842	0.0549	0.0356	0.0230	0.0148	0.0015	0.0001	0.0000	0.0000	0.0000	0.0000	0.0000	0.0000	0
1	0.9393	0.8095	0.6615	0.5210	0.3991	0.2990	0.2201	0.1594	0.1140	0.0805	0.0121	0.0015	0.0001	0.0000	0.0000	0.0000	0.0000	0.0000	1
2	0.9925	0.9543	0.8822	0.7855	0.6767	0.5665	0.4625	0.3694	0.2894	0.2228	0.0486	0.0079	0.0010	0.0001	0.0000	0.0000	0.0000	0.0000	2
3	0.9993	0.9918	0.9686	0.9252	0.8619	0.7827	0.6937	0.6007	0.5092	0.4231	0.1302	0.0285	0.0047	0.0006	0.0001	0.0000	0.0000	0.0000	3
4	1.0000	0.9988	0.9933	0.9790	0.9520	0.9104	0.8546	0.7868	0.7103	0.6290	0.2633	0.0759	0.0160	0.0026	0.0003	0.0000	0.0000	0.0000	4
5		0.9999	0.9988	0.9951	0.9861	0.9691	0.9419	0.9033	0.8535	0.7937	0.4325	0.1613	0.0433	0.0086	0.0013	0.0001	0.0000	0.0000	5
6		1.0000	0.9998	0.9990	0.9966	0.9909	0.9801	0.9624	0.9361	0.9005	0.6067	0.2859	0.0962	0.0238	0.0044	0.0006	0.0001	0.0000	6
7			1.0000	0.9998	0.9993	0.9977	0.9942	0.9873	0.9758	0.9581	0.7559	0.4371	0.1820	0.0553	0.0124	0.0021	0.0002	0.0000	7
8				1.0000	0.9999	0.9995	0.9985	0.9963	0.9919	0.9845	0.8646	0.5931	0.2998	0.1110	0.0303	0.0061	0.0009	0.0001	8
9					1.0000	0.9999	0.9997	0.9990	0.9976	0.9949	0.9328	0.7318	0.4395	0.1959	0.0644	0.0156	0.0027	0.0003	9
10						1.0000	0.9999	0.9998	0.9994	0.9985	0.9701	0.8392	0.5839	0.3087	0.1215	0.0352	0.0074	0.0011	10
11							1.0000	1.0000	0.9999	0.9996	0.9880	0.9125	0.7151	0.4406	0.2053	0.0709	0.0179	0.0032	11
12									1.0000	0.9999	0.9957	0.9568	0.8209	0.5772	0.3143	0.1285	0.0386	0.0083	12
13										1.0000	0.9986	0.9806	0.8968	0.7032	0.4408	0.2112	0.0751	0.0192	13
14											0.9996	0.9921	0.9456	0.8074	0.5721	0.3174	0.1326	0.0403	14
15											0.9999	0.9971	0.9738	0.8849	0.6946	0.4402	0.2142	0.0769	15
16											1.0000	0.9990	0.9884	0.9367	0.7978	0.5681	0.3185	0.1341	16
17												0.9997	0.9953	0.9680	0.8761	0.6885	0.4391	0.2148	17
18												0.9999	0.9983	0.9852	0.9301	0.7911	0.5651	0.3179	18
19												1.0000	0.9994	0.9937	0.9637	0.8702	0.6844	0.4373	19
20													0.9998	0.9976	0.9827	0.9256	0.7870	0.5627	20
21													1.0000	0.9991	0.9925	0.9608	0.8669	0.6821	21
22														0.9997	0.9970	0.9811	0.9233	0.7852	22
23														0.9999	0.9989	0.9917	0.9595	0.8659	23
24														1.0000	0.9996	0.9966	0.9804	0.9231	24
25															0.9999	0.9988	0.9914	0.9597	25
26															1.0000	0.9996	0.9966	0.9808	26
27																0.9999	0.9988	0.9917	27
28																1.0000	0.9996	0.9968	28
29																	0.9999	0.9989	29
30																	1.0000	0.9997	30
31																		0.9999	31
32																		1.0000	32

Table 1 Cumulative binomial distribution function (cont.)

x	p=0.01	0.02	0.03	0.04	0.05	0.06	0.07	0.08	0.09	0.10	0.15	0.20	0.25	0.30	0.35	0.40	0.45	0.50	x
n = 50 0	0.6050	0.3642	0.2181	0.1299	0.0769	0.0453	0.0266	0.0155	0.0090	0.0052	0.0003	0.0000	0.0000	0.0000	0.0000	0.0000	0.0000	0.0000	0
1	0.9106	0.7358	0.5553	0.4005	0.2794	0.1900	0.1265	0.0827	0.0532	0.0338	0.0029	0.0002	0.0000	0.0000	0.0000	0.0000	0.0000	0.0000	1
2	0.9862	0.9216	0.8108	0.6767	0.5405	0.4162	0.3108	0.2260	0.1605	0.1117	0.0142	0.0013	0.0001	0.0000	0.0000	0.0000	0.0000	0.0000	2
3	0.9984	0.9822	0.9372	0.8609	0.7604	0.6473	0.5327	0.4253	0.3303	0.2503	0.0460	0.0057	0.0005	0.0000	0.0000	0.0000	0.0000	0.0000	3
4	0.9999	0.9968	0.9832	0.9510	0.8964	0.8206	0.7290	0.6290	0.5277	0.4312	0.1121	0.0185	0.0021	0.0002	0.0000	0.0000	0.0000	0.0000	4
5	1.0000	0.9995	0.9963	0.9856	0.9622	0.9224	0.8650	0.7919	0.7072	0.6161	0.2194	0.0480	0.0070	0.0007	0.0001	0.0000	0.0000	0.0000	5
6		0.9999	0.9993	0.9964	0.9882	0.9711	0.9417	0.8981	0.8404	0.7702	0.3613	0.1034	0.0194	0.0025	0.0002	0.0000	0.0000	0.0000	6
7		1.0000	0.9999	0.9992	0.9968	0.9906	0.9780	0.9562	0.9232	0.8779	0.5188	0.1904	0.0453	0.0073	0.0008	0.0001	0.0000	0.0000	7
8			1.0000	0.9999	0.9992	0.9973	0.9927	0.9833	0.9672	0.9421	0.6681	0.3073	0.0916	0.0183	0.0025	0.0002	0.0000	0.0000	8
9				1.0000	0.9998	0.9993	0.9978	0.9944	0.9875	0.9755	0.7911	0.4437	0.1637	0.0402	0.0067	0.0008	0.0001	0.0000	9
10					1.0000	0.9998	0.9994	0.9983	0.9957	0.9906	0.8801	0.5836	0.2622	0.0789	0.0160	0.0022	0.0002	0.0000	10
11						1.0000	0.9999	0.9995	0.9987	0.9968	0.9372	0.7107	0.3816	0.1390	0.0342	0.0057	0.0006	0.0000	11
12							1.0000	0.9999	0.9996	0.9990	0.9699	0.8139	0.5110	0.2229	0.0661	0.0133	0.0018	0.0002	12
13								1.0000	0.9999	0.9997	0.9868	0.8894	0.6370	0.3279	0.1163	0.0280	0.0045	0.0005	13
14									1.0000	0.9999	0.9947	0.9393	0.7481	0.4468	0.1878	0.0540	0.0104	0.0013	14
15										1.0000	0.9981	0.9692	0.8369	0.5692	0.2801	0.0955	0.0220	0.0033	15
16											0.9993	0.9856	0.9017	0.6839	0.3889	0.1561	0.0427	0.0077	16
17											0.9998	0.9937	0.9449	0.7822	0.5060	0.2369	0.0765	0.0164	17
18											0.9999	0.9975	0.9713	0.8594	0.6216	0.3356	0.1273	0.0325	18
19											1.0000	0.9991	0.9861	0.9152	0.7264	0.4465	0.1974	0.0595	19
20												0.9997	0.9937	0.9522	0.8139	0.5610	0.2862	0.1013	20
21												0.9999	0.9974	0.9749	0.8813	0.6701	0.3900	0.1611	21
22												1.0000	0.9990	0.9877	0.9290	0.7660	0.5019	0.2399	22
23													0.9996	0.9944	0.9604	0.8438	0.6134	0.3359	23
24													0.9999	0.9976	0.9793	0.9022	0.7160	0.4439	24
25													1.0000	0.9991	0.9900	0.9427	0.8034	0.5561	25
26														0.9997	0.9955	0.9686	0.8721	0.6641	26
27														0.9999	0.9981	0.9840	0.9220	0.7601	27
28														1.0000	0.9993	0.9924	0.9556	0.8389	28
29															0.9997	0.9966	0.9765	0.8987	29
30															0.9999	0.9986	0.9884	0.9405	30
31															1.0000	0.9995	0.9947	0.9675	31
32																0.9998	0.9978	0.9836	32
33																0.9999	0.9991	0.9923	33
34																1.0000	0.9997	0.9967	34
35																	0.9999	0.9987	35
36																	1.0000	0.9995	36
37																		0.9998	37
38																		1.0000	38

Table 8 Critical values of the product moment correlation coefficient

The table gives the critical values, for different significance levels, of the product moment correlation coefficient, *r*, for varying sample sizes, *n*.

One tail Two tail	10% 20%	5% 10%	2.5% 5%	1% 2%	0.5% 1%	One tail Two tail
n						*n*
4	0.8000	0.9000	0.9500	0.9800	0.9900	4
5	0.6870	0.8054	0.8783	0.9343	0.9587	5
6	0.6084	0.7293	0.8114	0.8822	0.9172	6
7	0.5509	0.6694	0.7545	0.8329	0.8745	7
8	0.5067	0.6215	0.7067	0.7887	0.8343	8
9	0.4716	0.5822	0.6664	0.7498	0.7977	9
10	0.4428	0.5494	0.6319	0.7155	0.7646	10
11	0.4187	0.5214	0.6021	0.6851	0.7348	11
12	0.3981	0.4973	0.5760	0.6581	0.7079	12
13	0.3802	0.4762	0.5529	0.6339	0.6835	13
14	0.3646	0.4575	0.5324	0.6120	0.6614	14
15	0.3507	0.4409	0.5140	0.5923	0.6411	15
16	0.3383	0.4259	0.4973	0.5742	0.6226	16
17	0.3271	0.4124	0.4821	0.5577	0.6055	17
18	0.3170	0.4000	0.4683	0.5425	0.5897	18
19	0.3077	0.3887	0.4555	0.5285	0.5751	19
20	0.2992	0.3783	0.4438	0.5155	0.5614	20
21	0.2914	0.3687	0.4329	0.5034	0.5487	21
22	0.2841	0.3598	0.4227	0.4921	0.5368	22
23	0.2774	0.3515	0.4132	0.4815	0.5256	23
24	0.2711	0.3438	0.4044	0.4716	0.5151	24
25	0.2653	0.3365	0.3961	0.4622	0.5052	25
26	0.2598	0.3297	0.3882	0.4534	0.4958	26
27	0.2546	0.3233	0.3809	0.4451	0.4869	27
28	0.2497	0.3172	0.3739	0.4372	0.4785	28
29	0.2451	0.3115	0.3673	0.4297	0.4705	29
30	0.2407	0.3061	0.3610	0.4226	0.4629	30
31	0.2366	0.3009	0.3550	0.4158	0.4556	31
32	0.2327	0.2960	0.3494	0.4093	0.4487	32
33	0.2289	0.2913	0.3440	0.4032	0.4421	33
34	0.2254	0.2869	0.3388	0.3972	0.4357	34
35	0.2220	0.2826	0.3338	0.3916	0.4296	35
36	0.2187	0.2785	0.3291	0.3862	0.4238	36
37	0.2156	0.2746	0.3246	0.3810	0.4182	37
38	0.2126	0.2709	0.3202	0.3760	0.4128	38
39	0.2097	0.2673	0.3160	0.3712	0.4076	39
40	0.2070	0.2638	0.3120	0.3665	0.4026	40
41	0.2043	0.2605	0.3081	0.3621	0.3978	41
42	0.2018	0.2573	0.3044	0.3578	0.3932	42
43	0.1993	0.2542	0.3008	0.3536	0.3887	43
44	0.1970	0.2512	0.2973	0.3496	0.3843	44
45	0.1947	0.2483	0.2940	0.3457	0.3801	45
46	0.1925	0.2455	0.2907	0.3420	0.3761	46
47	0.1903	0.2429	0.2876	0.3384	0.3721	47
48	0.1883	0.2403	0.2845	0.3348	0.3683	48
49	0.1863	0.2377	0.2816	0.3314	0.3646	49
50	0.1843	0.2353	0.2787	0.3281	0.3610	50
60	0.1678	0.2144	0.2542	0.2997	0.3301	60
70	0.1550	0.1982	0.2352	0.2776	0.3060	70
80	0.1448	0.1852	0.2199	0.2597	0.2864	80
90	0.1364	0.1745	0.2072	0.2449	0.2702	90
100	0.1292	0.1654	0.1966	0.2324	0.2565	100

Table 9 Critical values of Spearman's rank correlation coefficient

The table gives the critical values, for different significance levels, of Spearman's rank correlation coefficient, r_s, for varying sample sizes, n.

Since r_s is discrete, exact significance levels cannot be obtained in most cases.

The critical values given are those with significance levels closest to the stated value.

One tail Two tail	10% 20%	5% 10%	2.5% 5%	1% 2%	0.5% 1%	One tail Two tail
n						*n*
4	1.0000	1.0000	1.0000	1.0000	1.0000	4
5	0.7000	0.9000	0.9000	1.0000	1.0000	5
6	0.6571	0.7714	0.8286	0.9429	0.9429	6
7	0.5714	0.6786	0.7857	0.8571	0.8929	7
8	0.5476	0.6429	0.7381	0.8095	0.8571	8
9	0.4833	0.6000	0.6833	0.7667	0.8167	9
10	0.4424	0.5636	0.6485	0.7333	0.7818	10
11	0.4182	0.5273	0.6091	0.7000	0.7545	11
12	0.3986	0.5035	0.5874	0.6713	0.7273	12
13	0.3791	0.4780	0.5604	0.6484	0.6978	13
14	0.3670	0.4593	0.5385	0.6220	0.6747	14
15	0.3500	0.4429	0.5179	0.6000	0.6536	15
16	0.3382	0.4265	0.5029	0.5824	0.6324	16
17	0.3271	0.4124	0.4821	0.5577	0.6055	17
18	0.3170	0.4000	0.4683	0.5425	0.5897	18
19	0.3077	0.3887	0.4555	0.5285	0.5751	19
20	0.2992	0.3783	0.4438	0.5155	0.5614	20
21	0.2914	0.3687	0.4329	0.5034	0.5487	21
22	0.2841	0.3598	0.4227	0.4921	0.5368	22
23	0.2774	0.3515	0.4132	0.4815	0.5256	23
24	0.2711	0.3438	0.4044	0.4716	0.5151	24
25	0.2653	0.3365	0.3961	0.4622	0.5052	25
26	0.2598	0.3297	0.3882	0.4534	0.4958	26
27	0.2546	0.3233	0.3809	0.4451	0.4869	27
28	0.2497	0.3172	0.3739	0.4372	0.4785	28
29	0.2451	0.3115	0.3673	0.4297	0.4705	29
30	0.2407	0.3061	0.3610	0.4226	0.4629	30
31	0.2366	0.3009	0.3550	0.4158	0.4556	31
32	0.2327	0.2960	0.3494	0.4093	0.4487	32
33	0.2289	0.2913	0.3440	0.4032	0.4421	33
34	0.2254	0.2869	0.3388	0.3972	0.4357	34
35	0.2220	0.2826	0.3338	0.3916	0.4296	35
36	0.2187	0.2785	0.3291	0.3862	0.4238	36
37	0.2156	0.2746	0.3246	0.3810	0.4182	37
38	0.2126	0.2709	0.3202	0.3760	0.4128	38
39	0.2097	0.2673	0.3160	0.3712	0.4076	39
40	0.2070	0.2638	0.3120	0.3665	0.4026	40
41	0.2043	0.2605	0.3081	0.3621	0.3978	41
42	0.2018	0.2573	0.3044	0.3578	0.3932	42
43	0.1993	0.2542	0.3008	0.3536	0.3887	43
44	0.1970	0.2512	0.2973	0.3496	0.3843	44
45	0.1947	0.2483	0.2940	0.3457	0.3801	45
46	0.1925	0.2455	0.2907	0.3420	0.3761	46
47	0.1903	0.2429	0.2876	0.3384	0.3721	47
48	0.1883	0.2403	0.2845	0.3348	0.3683	48
49	0.1863	0.2377	0.2816	0.3314	0.3646	49
50	0.1843	0.2353	0.2787	0.3281	0.3610	50
60	0.1678	0.2144	0.2542	0.2997	0.3301	60
70	0.1550	0.1982	0.2352	0.2776	0.3060	70
80	0.1448	0.1852	0.2199	0.2597	0.2864	80
90	0.1364	0.1745	0.2072	0.2449	0.2702	90
100	0.1292	0.1654	0.1966	0.2324	0.2565	100

Table 10 Critical values of the Wilcoxon signed-rank statistic

The table gives the lower tail critical values of the statistic T.

The upper tail critical values are given by $\frac{1}{2}n(n+1) - T$.

T is the sum of the ranks of observations with the same sign.
Since T is discrete, exact significance levels cannot usually be obtained.
The critical values tabulated are those with significance levels closest to the stated value.
The critical region includes the tabulated value.

One tail Two tail	10% 20%	5% 10%	2.5% 5%	1% 2%	0.5% 1%
n					
3	0				
4	1	0			
5	2	1	0		
6	4	2	1	0	
7	6	4	2	0	0
8	8	6	4	2	0
9	11	8	6	3	2
10	14	11	8	5	3
11	18	14	11	7	5
12	22	17	14	10	7
13	26	21	17	13	10
14	31	26	21	16	13
15	37	30	25	20	16
16	42	36	30	24	19
17	49	41	35	28	23
18	55	47	40	33	28
19	62	54	46	38	32
20	70	60	52	43	37

Table 11 Critical values of the Mann–Whitney U statistic

The table gives the lower tail critical values of the statistic U.

The upper tail critical values are given by $mn - U$.

$U = T - \dfrac{n(n + 1)}{2}$ where T is the sum of the ranks of the sample of size n.

Since T is discrete, exact significance levels cannot be obtained.
The critical values tabulated are those with significance levels closest to the stated value.
The critical region includes the tabulated value.

One tail 5% Two tail 10% n / m	2	3	4	5	6	7	8	9	10	11	12
2		0	0	0	0	1	1	1	2	2	2
3	0	0	1	1	2	3	3	4	5	5	6
4	0	1	2	3	4	5	6	7	8	9	10
5	0	1	3	4	5	7	8	10	11	12	14
6	0	2	4	5	7	9	11	12	14	16	18
7	1	3	5	7	9	11	13	15	18	20	22
8	1	3	6	8	11	13	16	18	21	24	26
9	1	4	7	10	12	15	18	21	24	27	30
10	2	5	8	11	14	18	21	24	28	31	34
11	2	5	9	12	16	20	24	27	31	35	39
12	2	6	10	14	18	22	26	30	34	39	43

One tail 2.5% Two tail 5% n / m	2	3	4	5	6	7	8	9	10	11	12
2				0	0	0	0	0	1	1	1
3			0	0	1	2	2	3	3	4	4
4		0	1	2	2	3	4	5	6	7	8
5	0	0	2	3	4	5	6	7	9	10	11
6	0	1	2	4	5	7	8	10	12	13	15
7	0	2	3	5	7	9	11	13	15	17	18
8	0	2	4	6	8	11	13	15	18	20	22
9	0	3	5	7	10	13	15	18	21	23	26
10	1	3	6	9	12	15	18	21	24	27	30
11	1	4	7	10	13	17	20	23	27	30	34
12	1	4	8	11	15	18	22	26	30	34	38

Answers

1 Further probability

EXERCISE 1A

1 (a) $\frac{19}{60}$; (b) $\frac{5}{12}$; (c) $\frac{1}{5}$; (d) $\frac{7}{12}$; (e) $\frac{8}{15}$; (f) $\frac{7}{12}$; (g) $\frac{1}{10}$.

2 $P(A \cup B) = \frac{21}{25} + \frac{15}{25} - \frac{13}{25} = \frac{23}{25} = 0.92$.

3 (a) $\frac{2}{5}$; (b) $\frac{1}{10}$; (c) $\frac{8}{15}$; (d) 0; (e) $\frac{3}{10}$; (f) $\frac{2}{15}$.

4 (a) $\frac{9}{100} = 0.09$;   (b) only $(1, 0)$ $\frac{1}{100} = 0.01$;
  (c) $\frac{9}{100} + \frac{4}{100} - \frac{1}{100} = \frac{12}{100} = 0.12$.

5 (a) $P(A \cap G) = \frac{20}{200} = \frac{1}{10} = 0.1$;
  (b) $P(A \cup G) = \frac{2}{5} + \frac{1}{5} - \frac{1}{10} = \frac{1}{2} = 0.5$;
  (c) $A \cap G$ is the event that a male who wears glasses is chosen.
  $A \cup G$ is the event that the worker chosen is either male or wears glasses, or both.

EXERCISE 1B

1 (a) $0.6 \times 0.9 \times 0.7 = 0.378$;
  (b) $(0.6 \times 0.1 \times 0.3) + (0.4 \times 0.9 \times 0.3) + (0.4 \times 0.1 \times 0.7) = 0.154$.

2 (a) $0.35 \times 0.35 \times 0.35 = 0.0429$;
  (b) $(0.0429) + (0.45 \times 0.45 \times 0.45) + (0.2 \times 0.2 \times 0.2) = 0.142$;
  (c) $(0.35 \times 0.45 \times 0.45) + (0.45 \times 0.35 \times 0.45) + (0.45 \times 0.45 \times 0.35)$
      $= 0.213$.

3 (a) $0.5 \times 0.3 \times 0.8 = 0.12$;
  (b) $0.5 \times 0.7 \times 0.2 = 0.07$;
  (c) $(0.5 \times 0.3 \times 0.8) + (0.5 \times 0.7 \times 0.8) + (0.5 \times 0.3 \times 0.2) = 0.43$.

4 (a) $0.2 \times 0.08 \times 0.05 = 0.0008$;
  (b) $0.2 \times 0.92 \times 0.95 = 0.175$;
  (c) $(0.2 \times 0.92 \times 0.95) + (0.8 \times 0.08 \times 0.95) + (0.8 \times 0.92 \times 0.05)$
      $= 0.272$;
  (d) $0.8 \times 0.92 \times 0.95 = 0.699$.

5 (a) $0.88 \times 0.94 \times 0.83 = 0.687$;
  (b) $0.88 \times 0.94 \times 0.17 = 0.141$;
  (c) $(0.88 \times 0.06 \times 0.17) + (0.12 \times 0.94 \times 0.17) + (0.12 \times 0.06 \times 0.83)$
      $= 0.0341$.

EXERCISE 1C

1 (a) $(0.95 \times 0.03) + (0.05 \times 0.96) = 0.0765$;
  (b) $\dfrac{(0.05 \times 0.96)}{0.0765} = 0.627$;
  (c) $(0.95 \times 0.97) + (0.05 \times 0.96) = 0.9695$.

2 (a) $0.4 \times 0.2 \times 0.2 \times 0.3 = 0.0048$;

(b) $0.6 \times 0.8 \times 0.8 \times 0.7 = 0.269$;

(c) $\left.\begin{array}{l} 0.4 \times 0.8 \times 0.8 \times 0.7 \\ 0.6 \times 0.2 \times 0.8 \times 0.7 \\ 0.6 \times 0.8 \times 0.2 \times 0.7 \\ 0.6 \times 0.8 \times 0.8 \times 0.3 \end{array}\right\} + = 0.429$;

(d) $0.4 \times 0.6 = 0.24$; **(e)** $0.6 \times 0.1 = 0.06$;

(f) $0.24 \times 0.06 = 0.30$; **(g)** $\dfrac{0.06}{0.30} = 0.2$.

3 (a) $(\frac{1}{7})^3 = \frac{1}{343} = 0.00292$; **(b)** $7 \times \frac{1}{343} = \frac{1}{49} = 0.0204$;

(c) $\frac{7}{7} \times \frac{6}{7} \times \frac{5}{7} = \frac{30}{49} = 0.612$; **(d)** $(\frac{2}{7})^3 = \frac{8}{343} = 0.0233$;

(e) $2 \times \dfrac{(\frac{1}{7})^3}{(\frac{2}{7})^3} = \dfrac{\frac{2}{343}}{\frac{8}{343}} = \frac{1}{4} = 0.25$.

4 (a) (i) $\frac{50}{125} = 0.4$, **(ii)** $\frac{28}{125} = 0.224$,

(iii) $\frac{118}{125} = 0.944$, **(iv)** $\frac{7}{20} = 0.35$;

(b) (i) C since $P(A \cap C) = \frac{13}{25} \neq P(A) \times P(C) = \frac{8}{125}$,

(ii) B since $P(A \cap B) = \frac{28}{125} = P(A) \times P(B) = \frac{28}{125}$,

(iii) A';

(c) (i) $(\frac{90}{100} \times \frac{70}{125}) + (\frac{80}{100} \times \frac{20}{125}) + (\frac{30}{100} \times \frac{35}{125}) = \frac{179}{250} = 0.716$,

(ii) $\left(\dfrac{\frac{30}{100} \times \frac{35}{125}}{\frac{179}{250}} \right) = \frac{21}{179} = 0.117$.

5 (a) (i) 0.1, **(ii)** 0.24;

(b) 0.15; **(c)** 0.5;

(d) 0.1 (Albert) $+ 0.15$ (Belinda) $+ 0.05$ (Khalid) $+ 0.2 = 0.5$;

(e) 0.3.

6 (a) $\frac{23}{30} = 0.767$; **(b)** $\frac{119}{150} = 0.793$; **(c)** $\frac{31}{150} = 0.207$;

(d) 30; **(e)** Prob a female employee is weekly paid;

(f) $\dfrac{0.1}{0.2} = 0.5$.

7 (a) $0.7 \times 0.6 \times 0.9 = 0.378$;

(b) $B(3, 0.9)\ 0.243$;

(c) (i) $\frac{6}{25} \times 0.6 = 0.144$,

(ii) $(\frac{9}{25} \times 0.7) + (\frac{6}{25} \times 0.6) + (\frac{10}{25} \times 0.5) = 0.756$,

(iii) $\dfrac{(\frac{6}{25} \times 0.6)}{0.756} = 0.190$.

8 (a) (i) $(0.9)^3 = 0.729$,

(ii) $(0.9 \times 0.04 \times 0.06) \times 6 = 0.0130$;

(b) (i) $0.9 \times 0.01 = 0.009$,

(ii) $(0.9 \times 0.01) + (0.04 \times 0.24) + (0.06 \times 0.55) = 0.0516$,

(iii) $\dfrac{0.009}{0.0516} = 0.174$,

(iv) $\dfrac{0.9 \times 0.99}{(1 - 0.0516)} = 0.939$.

9 (a) **(i)** $(0.7)^3 = 0.343,$

(ii) $3 \times 0.7^2 \times 0.3 = 0.441;$

(b) **(i)** $0.3 \times 0.3 \times 0.7 = 0.063,$

(ii) $0.3^2 = 0.09;$

(c) $(0.7 \times 0.8) = 0.56$ correct, $(0.7 \times 0.2) = 0.14$ incorrect.
One of each $6 \times 0.56 \times 0.14 \times 0.3 = 0.141;$

(d) **(i)** Less than or equal to 1500 calls are answered,

(ii) B, E,

(iii) C and E or D and E,

(iv) B, C, D.

10 (a) **(i)** $\frac{9}{22} = 0.409,$

(ii) $\frac{6}{11} = 0.545,$

(iii) $\frac{2}{11} = 0.182,$

(iv) $\frac{4}{7} = 0.571;$

(b) **(i)** 0.0303,

(ii) 0.450,

(iii) 0.0348;

(c) **(i)** $(\frac{35}{110} \times 0.96) + (\frac{75}{110} \times 0.08) = 0.36,$

(ii) $\dfrac{\frac{35}{110} \times 0.96}{0.36} = 0.848.$

11 (a) $0.25 \times 0.5 \times 0.2 = 0.025;$

(b) $0.2 \times 0.75 = 0.150;$

(c) $(0.2 \times 0.72) + (0.3 \times 0.5) + (0.5 \times 0.8) = 0.7;$

(d) $\dfrac{0.2 \times 0.75}{0.7} = 0.214;$

(e) $(0.2) \times (0.25 \times 0.5 \times 0.8) = 0.02.$

2 Hypothesis testing

EXERCISE 2A

1 (a) 0.997;

(b) $H_0 \ \rho = 0,$ $H_1 \ \rho \neq 0,$ test statistic 0.997, $n = 10,$ 2 tail 5%,
critical value 0.632.
Reject $H_0,$ significant association between level and hardness.

2 (a) 0.787;

(b) $H_0 \ \rho = 0,$ $H_1 \ \rho > 0,$ test statistic 0.787, $n = 14,$ 1 tail 5%,
critical value 0.4575.
Reject $H_0,$ significant direct association between body mass and heart
mass.

3 (a) 0.784;

(b) $H_0 \ \rho = 0,$ $H_1 \ \rho \neq 0,$ test statistic 0.784, $n = 10,$ 2 tail 5%,
critical value 0.632.
Reject $H_0,$ significant association inflation and unemployment rate.

4 (a) 0.610;

(b) H_0 $\rho = 0$, H_1 $\rho \neq 0$, test statistic 0.610, $n = 15$, 2 tail 5%, critical value 0.514.
Reject H_0, significant association between items produced and average quality score.

5 (a)

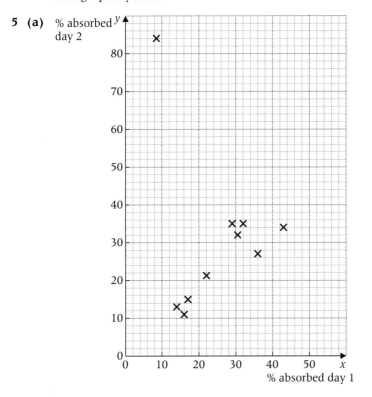

% absorbed day 2 (y-axis) vs % absorbed day 1 (x-axis)

(b) −0.118;

(c) H_0 $\rho = 0$, H_1 $\rho \neq 0$, test statistic −0.118, $n = 10$, 2 tail 5%, critical value 0.632.
Accept H_0, no significant association between % absorbed on first and second day.

(d) (i) patient 7,
 (ii) H_0 $\rho = 0$, H_1 $\rho \neq 0$, test statistic 0.863, $n = 9$, 2 tail 5%, critical value 0.666.
Accept H_0, significant association between % absorbed on first and second day.

6 (a) −0.944;

(b) H_0 $\rho = 0$, H_1 $\rho \neq 0$, test statistic −0.944, $n = 15$, 2 tail 1%, cv = 0.6411.
Reject H_0, significant association between latitude and mid-temperature.

EXERCISE 2B

1 Conclude there is a significant association between level of food supplement and shell hardness when no such association exists.

2 Conclude there is no direct association between body mass and heart mass when such an association does exist.

3 (a)

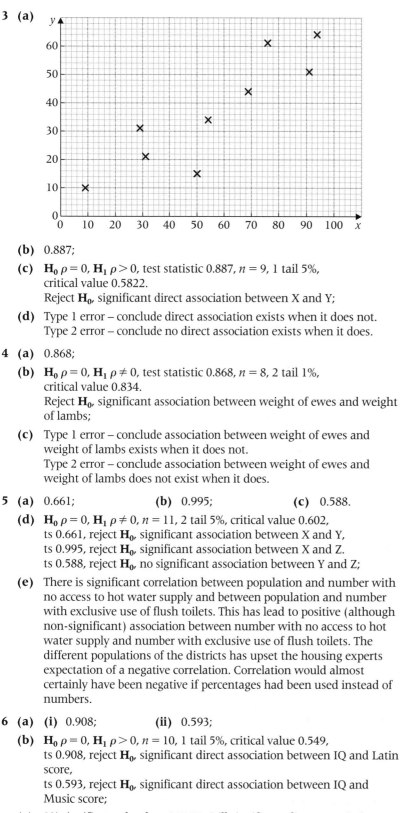

(b) 0.887;

(c) $H_0 \rho = 0$, $H_1 \rho > 0$, test statistic 0.887, $n = 9$, 1 tail 5%, critical value 0.5822.
Reject H_0, significant direct association between X and Y;

(d) Type 1 error – conclude direct association exists when it does not.
Type 2 error – conclude no direct association exists when it does.

4 (a) 0.868;

(b) $H_0 \rho = 0$, $H_1 \rho \neq 0$, test statistic 0.868, $n = 8$, 2 tail 1%, critical value 0.834.
Reject H_0, significant association between weight of ewes and weight of lambs;

(c) Type 1 error – conclude association between weight of ewes and weight of lambs exists when it does not.
Type 2 error – conclude association between weight of ewes and weight of lambs does not exist when it does.

5 (a) 0.661;   (b) 0.995;   (c) 0.588.

(d) $H_0 \rho = 0$, $H_1 \rho \neq 0$, $n = 11$, 2 tail 5%, critical value 0.602,
ts 0.661, reject H_0, significant association between X and Y,
ts 0.995, reject H_0, significant association between X and Z.
ts 0.588, reject H_0, no significant association between Y and Z;

(e) There is significant correlation between population and number with no access to hot water supply and between population and number with exclusive use of flush toilets. This has lead to positive (although non-significant) association between number with no access to hot water supply and number with exclusive use of flush toilets. The different populations of the districts has upset the housing experts expectation of a negative correlation. Correlation would almost certainly have been negative if percentages had been used instead of numbers.

6 (a) (i) 0.908;   (ii) 0.593;

(b) $H_0 \rho = 0$, $H_1 \rho > 0$, $n = 10$, 1 tail 5%, critical value 0.549,
ts 0.908, reject H_0, significant direct association between IQ and Latin score,
ts 0.593, reject H_0, significant direct association between IQ and Music score;

(c) 1% significance level, cv 0.7155. Still significant direct association between IQ and Latin but association between IQ and Music score not significant at 1%.

7 (a)

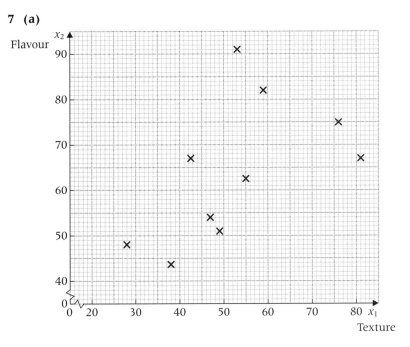

(b) 0.549;

(c) Scores less variable – more compact scatter diagram, no reason to expect change of overall pattern;

(d) H_0 $\rho = 0$, H_1 $\rho > 0$, $n = 10$, 1 tail 5%, critical value 0.5494, ts 0.858, reject H_0, conclude there is direct association between flavour and sweetness;

(e)

	X_1	X_2	X_3	X_4
X_1	1	0.549	0.232	−0.989
X_2		1	0.858	−0.478
X_3			1	−0.251
X_4				1

Omit X_4 because very strong (negative) linear relationship with X_1. Hence X_4 provides little additional information;

(f) 0.858.

8 (b) High amounts of nitrogen oxides associated with low amounts of carbon monoxide.
Relationship appears to be non-linear.
Most exhausts emit between 0.5 and 2.5 nitrogen oxides and between 2 and 16 carbon monoxide but there are some outliers, etc.
Suggestion not supported, scatter diagram suggests high nitrogen oxides associated with low carbon monoxide;

(c) −0.824;

(d) H_0 $\rho = 0$, H_1 $\rho \neq 0$, $n = 13$, 2 tail 1%, critical value 0.6835.
Reject H_0, significant association between X_1 and X_3;

(e) Fairly strong association (positive or negative) between Y and all the explanatory variables.
X_4 closely inversely related to X_2 but little sign of association with the other two explanatory variables, etc.

3 Rank correlation

EXERCISE 3A

1 0.750, fairly strong association between rank orders of preference and sweetness.

2 0.0952.   3 0.0500.

4 0.912, strong evidence that number of rotten peaches increases with number of days in storage.

5 (a) 0.922 (0.898 if $\sum d^2$ used);
   (b) Strong direct association between ranks of scores on the two questions.

6 (a) (i)   0.671 (0.673 if $\sum d^2$ used),
         (ii) 0.833,
         (iii) 0.958 (0.946 if $\sum d^2$ used);
   (b) Student L has very poor examination result but good practical grade and satisfactory essay grade;
   (c) Essay rank is very closely associated with practical work grade. Hence little information will be lost if essay rank no longer recorded;
   (d) PMCC cannot be calculated for letter grades.

EXERCISE 3B

1 (a) $H_0\ \rho_s = 0$, $H_1\ \rho_s \neq 0$, ts 0.0952, $n = 8$, cv 5%, two-tail test 0.7381.
        Accept H_0, no association between preference and price;
   (b) $H_0\ \rho_s = 0$, $H_1\ \rho_s > 0$, ts 0.750, $n = 7$, cv 1%, one-tail 0.8571.
        Accept H_0, no significant association between preference and sweetness;
   (c) $H_0\ \rho_s = 0$, $H_1\ \rho_s > 0$, ts 0.0500, $n = 9$, cv 1%, one-tail 0.7667.
        Accept H_0, no significant associations between colour and appearance;
   (d) $H_0\ \rho_s = 0$, $H_1\ \rho_s \neq 0$, ts 0.912, $n = 10$, cv 1%, two-tail 0.7818.
        Reject H_0, significant association between days in storage and number of rotten peaches.

2 −0.600.
   $H_0\ \rho_s = 0$, $H_1\ \rho_s < 0$, ts −0.600, $n = 5$, one-tail 5%, cv −0.900.
   Accept H_0, no significant association between judges' rankings.

3 0.444 (0.446 if $\sum d^2$ used).
   $H_0\ \rho_s = 0$, $H_1\ \rho_s \neq 0$, $n = 9$, cv 5%, two-tail 0.6833.
   Accept H_0, no significant association between takings and % part-time staff.

4 0.595.
   $H_0\ \rho_s = 0$, $H_1\ \rho_s \neq 0$, $n = 8$, cv 1%, two-tail 0.8571.
   Accept H_0, no significant association between reading age and rank of poem.

5 −0.798 (−0.783 if $\sum d^2$ used).
   $H_0\ \rho_s = 0$, $H_1\ \rho_s < 0$, $n = 9$, cv 5%, one-tail −0.6000.
   Reject H_0, significant inverse association between rainfall and sunshine.

MIXED EXERCISE

1 (b) 0.937;   (c) 0.973;
   (d) $H_0\ \rho = 0$, $H_1\ \rho \neq 0$, ts 0.937, $n = 11$, two-tail 1%, cv 0.7348.
        Reject H_0, significant evidence of association between maintenance cost and age.
        $H_0\ \rho_s = 0$, $H_1\ \rho_s \neq 0$, ts 0.973, $n = 11$, two-tail 1%, cv 0.7545.
        Reject H_0, significant evidence of association between ranks of maintenance cost and age.

2 (a) 0.745;

  (b) $H_0 \rho = 0$, $H_1 \rho > 0$, ts 0.745, $n = 10$, one-tail 5%, cv 0.5494.
  Reject H_0, significant direct association between IQ and English score;

  (c) −0.0952;

  (d) $H_0 \rho_s = 0$, $H_1 \rho_s \neq 0$, ts −0.0952, $n = 8$, two-tail 5%, cv 0.7381.
  Accept H_0, no significant association between ranks of aptitude and perseverance;

  (e) Students with high IQs tended to get high English scores, but perseverance did not appear to be related to aptitude.

3 (a) 0.861 (0.862 if $\sum d^2$ method used);

  (b) $H_0 \rho_s = 0$, $H_1 \rho_s > 0$, ts 0.861, $n = 12$, one-tail 5%, cv 0.5035.
  Reject H_0, significant direct association between ranks of training and service score ranks;

  (c) $H_0 \rho_s = 0$, $H_1 \rho_s \neq 0$, ts −0.808, $n = 12$, two-tail 5%, cv 0.5874.
  Reject H_0, significant (inverse) association between ranks of training and service score ranks.
  The training scores awarded by the second manager are (strangely) inversely associated with service scores. This manager appears to be a poor judge of how trainees will perform later when working for the company.

4 (a) Infant mortality

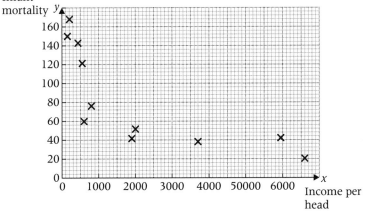

  (b) (i) −0.739,
     (ii) Scatter diagram shows relationship to be non-linear;

  (c) −0.936;

  (d) $H_0 \rho_s = 0$, $H_1 \rho_s \neq 0$, ts −0.936, $n = 11$, two-tail 1%, cv 0.7545.
  Reject H_0, evidence of significant inverse association between ranks of infant mortality and income;

  (e) Both correlation coefficients are negative but Spearman is numerically larger. This is because there is a strong but non-linear association between the variables as shown by the scatter diagram.

5 (a) (i) 0.899 (0.900 if $\sum d^2$ method used),
     (ii) 0.794;

  (b) $H_0 \rho_s = 0$, $H_1 \rho_s \neq 0$, ts 0.899, $n = 10$, two-tail 1%, cv 0.7818.
  Reject H_0, significant evidence of association between ranks of price and efficiency;

  (c) Appearance is associated with price but on this evidence not as strongly as efficiency is associated with price. Hence the appearance ranking provides useful additional information. Suggest if amount of data is to be reduced 'efficiency' should be dropped rather than 'appearance';

  (d) Not possible since efficiency grades are not numerical.

6 (a)

Gross
earnings
(£000)

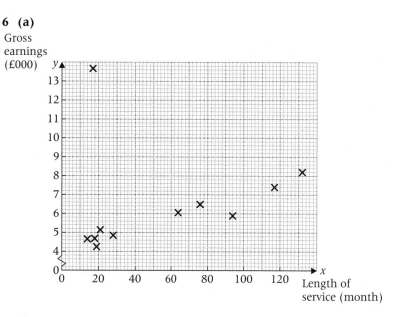

(b) 0.168;

(c) 0.518;

(d) $H_0 \; \rho_s = 0$, $H_1 \; \rho_s \neq 0$, ts 0.518, $n = 11$, two-tail 5%, cv 0.6091.
Accept H_0, no significant association between ranks of length of
service and gross earnings;

(e) Scatter diagram suggests that, apart from G who has short service
and the highest earnings, there is a tendency for earnings to increase,
approximately linearly, with length of service. Without the outlier (G)
the correlation coefficients would be close to 1. The outlier has
reduced the PMCC close to zero. It has also reduced Spearman's rank
correlation coefficient but not to the same extent.

7 (a)

Time (s)
right hand

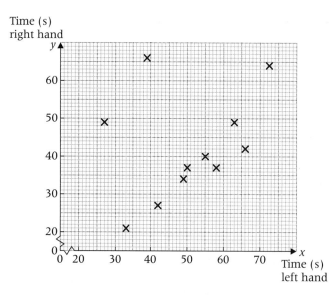

(b) 0.296;

(c) $H_0 \; \rho_s = 0$, $H_1 \; \rho_s \neq 0$, ts 0.296, $n = 11$, two-tail 5%, cv 0.6021.
Accept H_0, no evidence of significant positive association between
times with left and right hands;

(d) E and G since they were quicker with their left than with their right hand.   0.954.
$H_0 \rho_s = 0$, $H_1 \rho_s \neq 0$, ts 0.954, $n = 9$, two-tail 5%, cv 0.6833.
Reject H_0, evidence of significant positive association between times with left and right hands;

(e) Strong positive linear relationship between times taken with left and right hands when left handers excluded.

8 (a) 0.153, low value indicating little if any association;

(b) $H_0 \rho = 0$, $H_1 \rho \neq 0$, ts 0.153, $n = 8$, two-tail 5%, cv 0.7067.
Accept H_0, no significant evidence of association between X and Y;

(c) 0.738;

(d) $H_0 \rho_s = 0$, $H_1 \rho_s \neq 0$, ts 0.738, $n = 8$, two-tail 5%, cv 0.7381.
Reject H_0, evidence of significant positive association between number of adults with higher educational qualifications and size of population. (Note both test statistic and critical value round to 0.7381 and are for all practical purposes equal. The critical value is included in the critical region and so H_0 has been rejected (just).)

(e) W   7.93   4.96   6.60   3.07   15.23   7.59   7.29   12.83

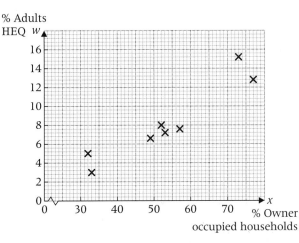

(f) There is a strong association between % with higher educational qualifications and % living in households in owner occupation. Because the different areas have very different sizes of population this association is not apparent between **number** with higher educational qualifications and % living in households in owner occupation.

9 (a)

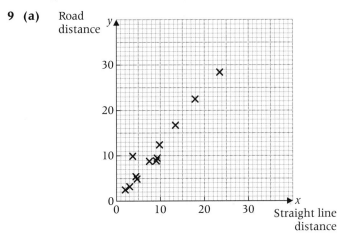

(b) F straight line distance exceeds road distance. Impossible – definitely an error. H road distance much longer than straight line distance. Unlikely but possible – probably an error;

(c) 0.406.
$H_0 \, \rho_s = 0$, $H_1 \, \rho_s \neq 0$, ts 0.406 (or -0.406 if shortest distance ranked 1), $n = 10$, two-tail 5%, cv 0.6845.
Accept H_0, no evidence of significant association between preference and ranked road distance;

10 (a) 0.232.
$H_0 \, \rho = 0$, $H_1 \, \rho \neq 0$, ts 0.232, $n = 6$, two-tail 5%, cv 0.8114.
Accept H_0, no significant evidence of association between estimates of Sonia and Jason;

(b) (i) -0.3,

(ii) Insufficient information,

(iii) Insufficient information,

(iv) -0.7.

11 (a) Index

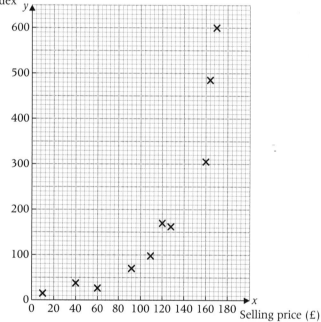

(b) 0.976;

(c) Relationship appears to be non-linear;

(d) ts 0.976, $n = 10$.

(i) $H_0 \, \rho_s = 0$, $H_1 \, \rho_s \neq 0$, 10%, two-tail, cv = 0.5636, reject H_0, conclude selling price associated with index,

(ii) $H_0 \, \rho_s = 0$, $H_1 \, \rho_s > 0$, 1%, one-tail, cv = 0.7333, reject H_0, conclude selling price positively associated with index,

(iii) $H_0 \, \rho_s = 0$, $H_1 \, \rho_s < 0$, 5%, one-tail, cv = -0.5636, accept H_0, no evidence to conclude high selling price associated with low value of index;

(e) Alternative hypothesis determines that the critical value will be negative. Since test statistic is positive null hypothesis must be accepted.

4 Non-parametric hypothesis tests – single sample

EXERCISE 4A

1 H_0 pop med = 135, H_1 pop med > 135.
One-tail 5%, $n = 14$, ts = 10^+ or 4^-.
$P(x \leq 4^-) = P(x \geq 10^+) = 0.0898 > 0.05$ (one-tail).
Accept H_0. Pop med = 135 ← no significant evidence to doubt.

2 H_0 pop med = 7.5, H_1 pop med $\neq$ 7.5.
Two-tail 5%, $n = 25$, ts = 7^+ or 18^-.
$P(x \leq 7^+) = P(x \geq 18^-) = 0.0216 < 0.025$ (two-tail).
Reject H_0. Significant evidence pop med, not 7.5 (lower).

3 H_0 pop med = 15, H_1 pop med < 15.
One-tail 1%, $n = 20$, ts = 3^+ or 17^-.
$P(x \leq 3^+) = P(x \geq 17^-) = 0.00129 < 0.01$ (one-tail).
Reject H_0. Significant evidence that pop med < 15.

4 H_0 pop med = 7.4, H_1 pop med > 7.4.
One-tail 5%, $n = 9$, ts = 7^+ or 2^-.
$P(x \geq 7^+) = P(x \leq 2^-) = 0.0898 > 0.05$ (one-tail).
Accept H_0. No significant evidence to doubt med = 7.4.

5 H_0 No difference in preference for sunflower and olive oil.
H_1 Sunflower preferred.
One-tail 5%, $n = 30$, ts = 20^+ or 10^-.
$P(x \geq 20^+) = P((x \leq 10^-) = 0.494 < 0.05$ (one-tail).
Reject H_0. Significant evidence that sunflower is preferred.

6 (a) H_0 population median = 52, H_1 population median > 52.
One-tail 1%, ts = 18^+ or 3^-.
$P(\geq 18^+) = P(\leq 3^-) = 0.000\,745 < 0.01$.
Reject H_0. Significant evidence that new recipe is preferred;

(b) Less than half preferred original flavour, accept original flavour **not** preferred without further calculation.

7 H_0 No difference H_1 A preferred   One-tail 5%.

(a) ts = 21^+ or 9^- ignore 2 zero $n = 30$.
$P(x \geq 21^+) = P(x \leq 9^-) = 0.0214 < 0.05$ (one-tail).
Reject H_0. Significant A better;

(b) Features randomly selected. Features equally important.
These are only relevant features to select car quality.

EXERCISE 4B

1 $T^- = 27\frac{1}{2}$, $T^+ = 77\frac{1}{2}$, H_0 Med/mean pop = 135, $n = 14$,
ts = $27\frac{1}{2}$,   cv = 26, H_1 Med/mean pop = 135,   one-tail 5%.
Accept H_0. No significant evidence to doubt med = 135.

2 $T^- = 9.5$, $T^+ = 35.5$, H_0 Med/mean pop = 7.4, $n = 9$,
ts = 9.5,   cv = 8, H_1 Med/mean pop > 7.4,   one-tail 5%.
Accept H_0. No significant evidence to doubt med = 7.4.

3 $T^- = 75$, $T^+ = 3$, H_0 Med/mean pop = 51, $n = 12$,
ts = 3,   cv = 10, H_1 Med/mean pop < 51,   one-tail 1%.
Reject H_0. Significant evidence that med/mean < 51.

4 $T^- = 59$, $T^+ = 151$, H_0 Med/mean pop = 23, $n = 20$,
ts = 59,   cv = 60, H_1 Med/mean pop > 23,   one-tail 5%.
Reject H_0. Significant evidence that med/mean > 23.

5 $T^- = 33$, $T^+ = 58$, H_0 Med/mean = 4, $n = 13$,
ts = 33,   cv = 21, H_1 Med/mean > 4,   one-tail 5%.
Accept H_0. No significant evidence to doubt med/mean = 4.

6 $T^- = 91$, $T^+ = 45$, $\mathbf{H_0}$ Med/mean $= \$95$, $n = 16$,
ts $= 45$, cv $= 30$, $\mathbf{H_1}$ Med/mean $\ne \$95$, two-tail 5%.
Accept $\mathbf{H_0}$. No significant evidence to doubt med/mean $= \$95$.

7 (a) $\mathbf{H_0}$ Med $= 30$, $\mathbf{H_1}$ Med < 30.
  $n = 20$, one-tail 5%, ts $= 5^+$ or 15^-,
  $P(\leqslant 5^+) = P(\leqslant 15^-) = 0.0207 < 0.05$ (one-tail).
  Reject $\mathbf{H_0}$. Significant evidence med < 30;

(b) $T^- = 135\frac{1}{2}$, $T^+ = 74\frac{1}{2}$, $\mathbf{H_0}$ Med/mean $= 30$, $\mathbf{H_1}$ Med/mean < 30,
  ts $= 74\frac{1}{2}$, cv $= 60$, $n = 20$, two-tail 5%.
  Accept $\mathbf{H_0}$. No evidence to conclude median isn't 30.

8 (a) $\mathbf{H_0}$ population median $= 200$, $\mathbf{H_1}$ population median > 200.
  Sign test $n = 20$, P(14 or more) $= 0.0577$, accept $\mathbf{H_0}$, no significant
  evidence that median life exceeds 200 hours;

(b) $\mathbf{H_0}$ population median $= 200$, $\mathbf{H_1}$ population median > 200.

Difference	-38	-21	-17	-16	-11	-5	10	15	25	34
	39	>40	>40	>40	>40	>40	>40	>40	>40	>40

Rank	-10	-7	-6	-5	-3	-1	2	4	8	9
	11	12	13	14	15	16	17	18	19	20

  ts $= 32$, cv for 1%, one-tailed test $= 43$.
  Reject $\mathbf{H_0}$ conclude median life greater than 200 hours;

(c) Sample random, distribution symmetrical;

(d) Would only know that 13 positive differences exceeded 12. Would
  not have been able to allocate signed ranks as four of the negative
  differences are numerically greater than 12.

9 (a) $\mathbf{H_0}$ population median $= 20$, $\mathbf{H_1}$ population median $\ne 20$.
  ts $= 13$, cv for 5%, two-tailed test $= 8$, accept $\mathbf{H_0}$ that mean external
  diameter is 20;

(b) $\mathbf{H_0}$ population median $= 20$, $\mathbf{H_1}$ population median $\ne 20$.
  ts $= 11$, cv for 5%, two-tailed test $= 8$, accept $\mathbf{H_0}$ that mean external
  diameter is 20;

(c) (i) null hypothesis in this case states the value of the median
    which will be accepted unless there is overwhelming evidence
    to disprove it,
  (ii) Type 1 error is concluding that the median is not 20 when in fact
    it is 20. (A Type 1 error cannot have been made in this example
    as the null hypothesis has been accepted in both cases.)
  (iii) Type 2 error is accepting that the median is 20 when in fact it
    is not 20. (At least one Type 2 error has been made in this
    example as the original measurements and the corrected
    measurements cannot both have a median of 20.)
    Accepting the null bypothesis is not the same as proving it is
    true. The technicians conclusions merely state that in neither
    case is there overwhelming evidence to reject the null hypothesis.

10 (a) $\mathbf{H_0}$ population median $= 12$, $\mathbf{H_1}$ population median > 12.
  $n = 30$, P(23 or more) $= 0.0026$. Reject $\mathbf{H_0}$, at 1% significance level,
  conclude average (as measured by median) annual number of visits
  to the cinema exceeds 12;

(b) (i) Conclusion unaffected, the sign test does not assume normal
    distribution,
  (ii) Conclusion unaffected, the sign test does not assume
    symmetrical distribution,
  (iii) Data biased as all interviewees had been to the cinema at least
    once. Conclusions completely unreliable.

11 (a) H_0 population median $= 2.9$, H_1 population median $\neq 2.9$.
$n = 20$, $p = 0.5$, P(5 or fewer > 2.9) + P(5 or fewer < 2.9) $= 0.0414$.
Reject H_0, conclude median weight less than 2.9 kg.

   (b) H_0 population median $= 2.9$, H_1 population median < 2.9.
$n = 23$, $p = 0.5$, P(5 or fewer) $= 0.0053$.
Reject H_0, conclude median weight less than 2.9 kg.

   (c) H_0 population median $= 2.9$, H_1 population median > 2.9.
Accept H_0, no need for calculation since more than half the lambs weight less than 2.9 kg and so there is no evidence at all to suggest median weight is greater than 2.9 kg.

5 Simple experimental design and paired tests

EXERCISE 5A

1 P(2 or fewer $+$) + P(2 or fewer $-$) $= 0.109$, no significant evidence of difference.

2 (a) Each student has a pair of times – one with audience, one without;

   (b) Differences between students are likely to be a major contributor to experimental error. This source is eliminated by using the differences in times for each student;

   (c) P(2 or fewer $+$) $= 0.0547$ evidence of longer times in front of audience not (quite) significant;

   (d) With audience always done after without audience. Order could effect result.
Population not defined, nor is method of selecting the sample.
Sample small – a larger sample might have lead to a significant difference.
Define population. Attempt to ensure unbiased sample (ideally random but this is unlikely to be possible).
Randomise order of tasks.

3 (a) Neither the subjects of the trial nor the staff administering the treatment know who is receiving the experimental treatment and who the placebo;

   (b) A placebo is a treatment which appears identical to the experimental treatment but contains no active ingredient;

   (c) P(1 or fewer $+$) $= 0.0352$ significant evidence that new preparation leads to greater improvement.

4 P(3 or fewer $+$) + P(3 or fewer $-$) $= 0.146$ no significant evidence of difference in load times.

5 P(2 or fewer $+$) $= 0.0193$ significant evidence that EPCSD is quicker. Need information on costs, availability, training requirements, attitude of workforce, etc. before making a decision.

EXERCISE 5B

1 (a) Paired design reduces experimental error, allocation at random reduces possibility of any difference found being due to order or change in conditions;

   (b) $T = 4$, cv $= 8$, significant evidence that athletes faster on synthetic track.

2 $T = 6.5$, cv $= 11$, significant evidence that students take longer with audience.

3 T = 1.5, cv = 2, significant evidence of greater improvement using new preparation.

4 T = 18, cv = 14, no significant evidence of difference.

5 (a) Reduces experimental error by eliminating differences between subjects, particularly useful in this case as differences between subjects appear to be large;

 (b) T = 15.5, cv = 4, no significant evidence of alcohol influencing blood clotting time;

6 T = 16.5, cv = 17, significant evidence less wear using leather A.

7 T = 8.5, cv = 10, significant evidence zinc concentration higher on river bed.

8 (a) (i) P(2 or fewer +) + P(3 or fewer −) = 0.109, no significant evidence of difference,

 (ii) T = 7, cv = 10, significant evidence pulse rate higher at 11 am;

 (b) Wilcoxon takes account of magnitude as well as sign of the differences and so is more likely to detect a difference if one exists.

9 (a) H_0 population median difference = 0
 H_1 population median difference > 0.

	Mon	Tue	Wed	Thur	Fri	Sat
New − Old	18	5	−6	−2	42	19

 T = 4, cv 1 for 5%, one-tailed test = 2.
 Accept H_0 conclude no difference between suppliers.

 (b) Takings will be affected by factors other than the supplier. This is known as experimental error. The difference found in Jim's original 1-day trial may be due to experimental error rather than to a difference between suppliers. In the analysis of Yasmin's trial the differences between takings on the same day of the week are analysed thus removing the effect of 'day' – a large source of experimental error. The analysis is based on more than one difference (replicates) thus allowing the size of the remaining experimental error to be taken into account. To remove the possibility of unconscious bias entering the experiment the order in which the two suppliers were used should be chosen at random.

10 (a) (i) H_0 population median difference = 0
 H_1 population median difference ≠ 0.
 n = 8, p = 0.5, P(5 or more +) + P(5 or more −) = 0.7266.
 Accept H_0 no difference in time to spoilage.

 (ii) H_0 population median difference = 0
 H_1 population median difference ≠ 0.
 T = 6, n = 7, cv for 5%, two-tailed test = 2.
 Accept H_0 no difference in time to spoilage.

 (b) Both tests assume the sample may be regarded as random.
 Valid to use all eight pairs for sign test. Magnitude of one difference unknown so cannot be included in Wilcoxon's test. This test is valid for the remaining seven differences provided it is reasonable to assume that the population is symmetrical.
 However neither test shows a significant difference.

 (c) Advantages of sign test – quicker and easier to collect data. Only necessary to observe which half of each pair spoils first – no need to assume population symmetrical.
 Advantage of Wilcoxon's test – more likely to detect a difference if such a difference exists.

11 (a) H_0 population median difference = 0
H_1 population median difference > 0.
$n = 14$, $p = 0.5$, P(9 or more +) = 0.2120.
Accept H_0 no significant difference in coursework and examination marks.

(b) Very little variation in coursework marks for those students who handed it in. Coursework marks only distinguish between those who handed in and the others.

(c) H_0 population median difference = 0,
H_1 population median difference > 0.
$n = 11$, $p = 0.5$, P(9 or more) = 0.0327.
Reject H_0 coursework marks significantly higher than examination marks on average.

(d) Those students who hand in coursework appear to all get about the same mark. This mark is higher, on average, than their examination marks. This difference disappears if all students are included in the analysis.

12 (a) H_0 population median difference = 0
H_1 population median difference > 0.
$n = 11$, $p = 0.5$, P(8 or more +) = 0.1133.
Accept H_0, proposal 2 not significantly better than proposal 1.

(b) Members of staff who read the proposals could be regarded as a random sample;

(c) H_0 population median difference = 0
H_1 population median difference ≠ 0.
T = 2, $n = 9$, cv for 5%, two-tail test = 6.
Reject H_0 proposal 2 better than proposal 1;

(d) Differences symmetrically distributed;

(e) No difference for sign test but Wilcoxon's signed-rank test could not have been carried out.

13 (a) H_0 population median difference = 0
H_1 population median difference ≠ 0.
T = 0, $n = 5$, cv 5%, two-tail test is 0.
Reject H_0 significant difference in median score on two rounds (4th round lower).

(b) 0.03125. **(c)** The probability of all signs being the same, if null hypothesis is true is 0.0625, hence not possible to reject null hypothesis at 5% level using the sign test whatever the scores.

(d) 7; **(e)** 7; **(f)** Population of differences symmetrical.

14 (a) H_0 population median difference = 0,
H_1 population median difference ≠ 0.
T = 6, $n = 8$, cv for 1%, two-tail test = 0.
Accept H_0 no significant difference between age at death of vegetarians and non-vegetarians.

(b) H_0 population median difference = 0
H_1 population median difference ≠ 0.
$n = 31$, $p = 0.5$, P(23 or more +) + P(23 or more −) = 0.0107.
Reject H_0 the vegetarians have lived longer.

(c) Advantage – magnitude of differences taken account of in the test. Disadvantage – n smaller because data on magnitude of differences for 23 pairs not yet available.

(d) Conclusion suggests vegetarians live longer but should be treated with caution because;
(i) only vegetarians who had already reached the age of 70 are considered,
(ii) pairs where both have survived five years are not considered.
Both these facts could have introduced bias.

6 The Mann–Whitney U test – unpaired samples

EXERCISE 6A

1 U = 35, cv = 27. Accept no significant differences in average times for girls and boys.
Random selection of subjects good. Similar numbers of boys and girls OK, but might have been better to arrange to have same number of each. Population is one age group at a particular school so conclusions only apply to this limited group.

2 U = 6.5, cv = 11. Significant evidence that premium batteries last longer on average.
There is no control over how the cars (batteries) are used. This may lead to substantial experimental error but no obvious reason why it should lead to bias.

3 U = 12.5, cv = 4. Accept no significant difference between average scores for boys and girls.

4 U = 14, cv = 13. Accept no significant difference between average scores on the two tests.
Experimental error is in this case the effect of factors other than different tests on the results. If there were no experimental error all the scores on a particular test would be the same.

5 Mann–Whitney, U = 15, cv = 15. Significant evidence plants grow faster, on average, on the west facing side.
Mann–Whitney can be used to compare two populations where the data is not paired.

6 U = 9, cv = 8. Accept no significant evidence of difference between oranges and lemons.

7 (a) Two independent samples, no natural pairing;
   (b) U = 4, cv = 5. Evidence of higher cost in Southville.

8 (a) Mann–Whitney, U = 19, cv = 8. Accept no significant difference in times;
   (b) If route is used regularly drivers are unlikely to lose their way, therefore reasonable to exclude this result as purpose is to compare times in normal use.

9 (a) U = 8, cv = 5. Accept no significant difference in miles driven on 4 gallons of petrol;
   (b) Good features – relatively cheap and easy to collect data.
        Bad features – samples self selecting – may involve bias,
                      – little opportunity to standardise driving conditions or ensure accuracy of data,
                      – no control over sample sizes.

10 (a) All oranges of variety P measured by inspector A and all variety B measured by inspector B. If each inspector had measured some of each, any systematic differences in their measurements could not have been confused with a difference between varieties of orange.
   (b) U = 24, cv = 27. Evidence of difference in average weights (P heavier).

11 (a) Mann–Whitney, U = 13, cv = 7. Accept no significant difference between average days to puncture;

(b) Good features – data easy and cheap to collect.
Bad features   – samples self selecting – may involve bias,
                 – little opportunity to check accuracy of data,
                 – distance cycled would be a more relevant variable
                   (although more difficult to obtain) than time,
                 – no control over sample sizes. A larger sample for B
                   would have given more chance of detecting a
                   difference if one exists.

(c) Type 1 error – concluding a difference between makes of tyres exists when it does not (cannot have been made in this case).
Type 2 error – accepting no difference between makes of tyre when one exists.

12 (a) Choose Wilcoxon's signed-rank test since both possible and Wilcoxon gives more chance of detecting a difference if one exists.
T = 1, cv = 0.
Evidence not significant at 1%. Accept mean time 210 seconds.

(b) U = 2, cv = 5.
Conclude assistant on average quicker than the engineer.

(c) Since there is a difference in average shaving times for different people, same person should test more than one type of razor. Standard and new design could both be used by several people and analysed using a paired comparison. Method of shaving and timing could also be standardised to further reduce experimental error.

13 (a) U = 11, cv = 11. Significant evidence creatinine levels measured by Analyser A are lower on average;

(b) T = 1, cv = 2. Significant evidence creatinine levels measured by Analyser A are lower;

(c) Since in second trial the same samples of blood were analysed, the lower measurements by Analyser A can no longer be explained by non-random differences between blood samples. However still unable to say which analyser is more accurate.

(d) Analyser A, T = 1.5, cv = 4. Significant evidence of bias.
Analyser B, T = 10, cv = 4. Accept mean is 90 – no significant evidence of bias.

(e) (i) Analyser B shown to be biased, suggests use A to avoid bias,
    (ii) Since all readings are on same sample low variability is desirable. Analyser A appears to be much more variable. Recommend use Analyser B after recalibration to remove bias.

14 (a) U = 16, cv = 21. Conclude significant evidence that apples of variety 2 are on average heavier than variety 1;

(b) No effect, rankings would still be the same;

(c) No effect, the evidence that variety 2 was heavier would be even stronger.

S3 Exam style practice paper

1 (a)

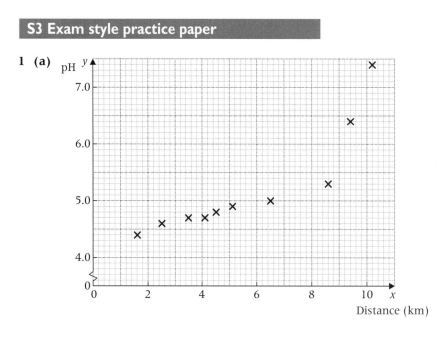

pH starts well below the desirable level and increases approximately linearly with distance from about 2 km to 8 km. It then apparently increases at a much faster rate with distance from about 8.5 km to 10 km. The final observation is just above the desirable level;

(b) 0.997;

(c) cv = ±0.6485. Significant association between ranks of distance and of pH values. Close to the factory the pH levels indicate acidity. They increase with distance and reach the desirable level at about 10 km from the factory. No data to indicate what happens beyond 10 km;

(d) The scatter diagram shows a non-linear relationship although the ranks of the data are in almost complete agreement. Product moment correlation coefficient will be less than Spearman's rank because of the non-linearity.

2 (a) Experimental error reduced by both modules being judged by the same students. More likely to detect a difference if a difference exists;

(b) T = 12.5, cv = 14. Conclude there is a significant difference – module 2 preferred;

(c) $P(\leqslant 2+) = 0.0193$. Conclude students have performed below expectation;

(d) Students appear to perform less well than average and so the result in **(b)** may not apply to a typical group of students.

3 (a) 0.044;

(b) 0.449;

(c) 0.0980;

(d) 0.918.

S6 Exam style practice paper

1 (a) 2+, P(2 or fewer +) + P(2 or fewer −) = 0.0004.
Significant evidence, at 1%, that median income in flats lower than in town;

(b) (i) No change – sign test makes no assumption about the shape of the distribution,

(ii) Samples not random – could completely change conclusions. In this case people at home on Tuesday morning likely to contain large proportion of pensioners and unemployed and so probably underestimates the median income.

2 (a) T = 13, cv = 4. Accept no difference;

(b) Good features – samples random.
Bad features　– people from one block of flats probably not representative of area as a whole,
　　　　　　– sample from Moss Side too small to give much chance of detecting a difference even if one exists.

3 (a) (i) 0.003375, **(ii)** 0.0574, **(iii)** 0.655, **(iv)** 0.0876;

(b) (i) B and C, **(ii)** B and D, **(iii)** B and E.

4 (a)

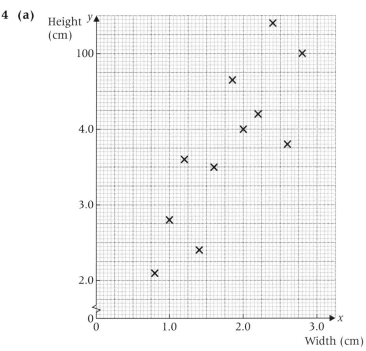

(b) (i) 1.8 0.663 (or 0.632), **(ii)** 3.75, 1.03 (or 0.977),
(iii) 0.824;

(c) cv = 0.5214. Evidence of positive association between length and width;

(d) First species length and width approximately linear with quite a lot of scatter, second species definitely non-linear but little scatter. This cannot be detected by summary statistics which are almost identical for both sets of data;

(e) Not appropriate since relationship non-linear.

Index